高职高专经济管理类创新教材

商务英语翻译实务

马国志 主　编

石奇宽 副主编

清华大学出版社
北　京

内容简介

本教材作者以常用商务文本为载体，构建了任务驱动、项目引领交替进行的商务文本翻译训练模式，指导学生进行典型文本的英汉翻译训练，高效完成商务文本翻译任务。考虑到岗位任务的实际操作，翻译练习以真实案例为情境，以英汉翻译为主，兼顾汉英翻译，训练难度适中，能够有效地培养学生的商务文本翻译能力。为贯彻落实党的二十大精神和各项教育方针，培养高素质技能人才，本教材每单元设置"聚焦价值引领"模块，引导学生坚定文化自信，培养国际视野、家国情怀和专业能力。

本教材适合高等职业院校商贸类专业的学生，也可供从事经贸翻译、国际贸易、国际会展、文化交流、涉外旅游等行业工作人员和英语自学者使用。

本书封面贴有清华大学出版社防伪标签，无标签者不得销售。
版权所有，侵权必究。举报：010-62782989，beiqinquan@tup.tsinghua.edu.cn。

图书在版编目(CIP)数据

商务英语翻译实务 / 马国志主编．—北京：清华大学出版社，2024.1
高职高专经济管理类创新教材
ISBN 978-7-302-64994-6

Ⅰ．①商… Ⅱ．①马… Ⅲ．①商务－英语－翻译－高等职业教育－教材 Ⅳ．① F7

中国国家版本馆 CIP 数据核字 (2023) 第 231213 号

责任编辑：刘远菁
封面设计：常雪影
版式设计：方加青
责任校对：马遥遥
责任印制：杨　艳

出版发行：清华大学出版社
网　　址：https://www.tup.com.cn，https://www.wqxuetang.com
地　　址：北京清华大学学研大厦 A 座　　邮　编：100084
社 总 机：010-83470000　　邮　购：010-62786544
投稿与读者服务：010-62776969，c-service@tup.tsinghua.edu.cn
质 量 反 馈：010-62772015，zhiliang@tup.tsinghua.edu.cn
印 装 者：三河市铭诚印务有限公司
经　　销：全国新华书店
开　　本：185mm×260mm　　印　张：14.25　　字　数：286 千字
版　　次：2024 年 1 月第 1 版　　印　次：2024 年 1 月第 1 次印刷
定　　价：59.00 元

产品编号：103230-01

前　言

　　《商务英语翻译实务》是依据《高等职业教育专科英语课程标准(2021年版)》(以下简称"新课标"),结合职业院校学生的岗位技能要求而编写的一部实训教材。本教材作者力求将商务翻译知识、技能培训与业务活动有机结合,引导学生探索商务文本的组织结构、文体特征和翻译要领,培养学生的商务文本英汉互译能力和跨文化交际能力。

　　本教材作者实地调研了外事外贸企业商务助理的岗位技能要求,针对高职高专商务英语翻译课程教学目标,结合高职院校学生的学习特点,确定以常用商务文本为载体,指导学生进行典型文本的英汉翻译训练,培养学生的商务文本翻译技能,力求产出准确、流畅的译文,高效完成商务文本翻译任务。

　　本教材具有如下特色。

1. 精选商务文本，教材结构合理

　　本教材作者针对外事外贸企业商务助理的岗位技能要求,构建了任务驱动、项目引领交替进行的商务文本翻译训练模式,能够有效提升职业院校学生的商务文本翻译能力。本书选材精当,结构合理,训练内容循序渐进,包括比较简单的商务文本,如名片、公示语、中西菜单、商业广告和求职文本;中等难度的商务文本,如旅游文本、企业简介、产品说明书和会展文本;难度很大的商务文本,如商务报告和商务合同。考虑到岗位任务的实际操作,翻译练习以真实案例为情境,以英汉翻译为主,兼顾汉英翻译,训练难度适中,能够有效地培养学生的商务文本翻译能力。

2. 注重翻译实践，有效提升技能

　　考虑到职业院校学生的英语基础,本教材作者阐述翻译理论知识时,采用简洁通俗、平实易懂的表达,引导学生掌握商务文本的翻译要领。本教材以商务文本为载体,指导学生进行商务文本翻译训练,探索翻译技能。每单元首先阐述商务文本的结构功能和文体特点(比较英汉文本的异同点),然后指导学生完成典型文本翻译任务,鼓励学生总结翻译思路和方法,接下来设置针对性强的文本翻译练习,从而巩固和提升学生的商务文本翻译能力。

3. 聚焦价值引领，树立远大理想

为贯彻落实党的二十大精神和各项教育方针，培养高素质技术技能人才，本教材每单元设置"聚焦价值引领"模块，引导学生坚定文化自信，树立为中华民族伟大复兴而不懈努力、贡献力量的理想信念。学生通过本教材进行商务文本翻译训练，既能提升商务文本的英汉互译能力，又能培养国际视野、家国情怀和专业能力。

《商务英语翻译实务》由天津商务职业学院马国志老师担任主编，天津壹触科技有限公司总经理石奇宽担任副主编。本教材是校企深度合作编写的一部商务文本翻译实训教材。本教材体现了"以就业为导向，以职业能力培养为核心"的人才培养理念，能够有效地提升职业院校学生和外经贸从业人员的商务文本翻译能力。

在编写教材的过程中，我们参考了众多国内外学者的翻译论著、商务英语翻译教材、商务英语写作教材和行业网站资料，在此向各位作者深表谢意。由于作者水平和时间所限，书中难免存在疏漏，敬请广大专家和读者批评、指正。反馈邮箱：wkservice@vip.163.com。

本教材免费提供习题答案及配套电子课件，授课教师扫描下方二维码并填写相关验证信息即可下载。

作者

2023年7月

目 录

Unit One 商务翻译基础 Essentials of Business Translation ········ 1

热身练习 Warm-up Exercises ·· 2
商务翻译概述 Overview of Business Translation ································· 3
熟悉文本特征 Learn about Stylistic Features ······································ 5
文本翻译实践 Do the Text Translation ·· 9
探索翻译技能 Explore Translation Skills ·· 11
巩固翻译技能 Enhance Translation Skills ·· 14
磨炼翻译技能 Sharpen Translation Skills ·· 15
拓展翻译技能 Broaden Translation Skills ·· 17
聚焦价值引领 Focus on Values Education ··· 20

Unit Two 商务名片 Business Card ·· 21

热身练习 Warm-up Exercises ·· 22
文本功能及构成 Structure and Functions ·· 23
熟悉文本特征 Learn about Stylistic Features ···································· 24
文本翻译实践 Do the Text Translation ·· 25
探索翻译技能 Explore Translation Skills ·· 27
巩固翻译技能 Enhance Translation Skills ·· 30
磨炼翻译技能 Sharpen Translation Skills ·· 31
拓展翻译技能 Broaden Translation Skills ·· 32
聚焦价值引领 Focus on Values Education ··· 33

Unit Three 公示语 Public Sign ·· 34

热身练习 Warm-up Exercises ·· 35
文本功能及构成 Structure and Functions ·· 36

熟悉文本特征 Learn about Stylistic Features ·· 37
文本翻译实践 Do the Text Translation ··· 38
探索翻译技能 Explore Translation Skills ·· 39
巩固翻译技能 Enhance Translation Skills ·· 41
磨炼翻译技能 Sharpen Translation Skills ·· 42
拓展翻译技能 Broaden Translation Skills ·· 43
聚焦价值引领 Focus on Values Education ··· 45

Unit Four 求职文本 Job-hunting Texts ·· 46

热身练习 Warm-up Exercises ··· 47
文本功能及构成 Structure and Functions ·· 49
熟悉文本特征 Learn about Stylistic Features ·· 50
文本翻译实践 Do the Text Translation ··· 51
探索翻译技能 Explore Translation Skills ·· 54
巩固翻译技能 Enhance Translation Skills ·· 59
磨炼翻译技能 Sharpen Translation Skills ·· 62
拓展翻译技能 Broaden Translation Skills ·· 63
聚焦价值引领 Focus on Values Education ··· 65

Unit Five 证明文本 Certificate ·· 66

热身练习 Warm-up Exercises ··· 67
文本功能及构成 Structure and Functions ·· 68
熟悉文本特征 Learn about Stylistic Features ·· 70
文本翻译实践 Do the Text Translation ··· 70
探索翻译技能 Explore Translation Skills ·· 72
巩固翻译技能 Enhance Translation Skills ·· 75
磨炼翻译技能 Sharpen Translation Skills ·· 76
拓展翻译技能 Broaden Translation Skills ·· 77
聚焦价值引领 Focus on Values Education ··· 78

目录

Unit Six 商业广告 Commercial ·· 79

热身练习 Warm-up Exercises ·································· 80
文本功能及构成 Structure and Functions ·················· 81
熟悉文本特征 Learn about Stylistic Features ··············· 81
文本翻译实践 Do the Text Translation ······················ 86
探索翻译技能 Explore Translation Skills ···················· 88
巩固翻译技能 Enhance Translation Skills ··················· 91
磨炼翻译技能 Sharpen Translation Skills ··················· 92
拓展翻译技能 Broaden Translation Skills ··················· 93
聚焦价值引领 Focus on Values Education ·················· 95

Unit Seven 中西菜单 Menu of Chinese/Western Food ·············· 96

热身练习 Warm-up Exercises ·································· 97
文本功能及构成 Structure and Functions ·················· 98
熟悉文本特征 Learn about Stylistic Features ··············· 99
文本翻译实践 Do the Text Translation ······················ 100
探索翻译技能 Explore Translation Skills ···················· 102
巩固翻译技能 Enhance Translation Skills ··················· 104
磨炼翻译技能 Sharpen Translation Skills ··················· 106
拓展翻译技能 Broaden Translation Skills ··················· 107
聚焦价值引领 Focus on Values Education ·················· 109

Unit Eight 旅游文本 Tourism Texts ································· 110

热身练习 Warm-up Exercises ·································· 111
文本功能及构成 Structure and Functions ·················· 112
熟悉文本特征 Learn about Stylistic Features ··············· 113
文本翻译实践 Do the Text Translation ······················ 115
探索翻译技能 Explore Translation Skills ···················· 117
巩固翻译技能 Enhance Translation Skills ··················· 120

磨炼翻译技能 Sharpen Translation Skills ················ 121
拓展翻译技能 Broaden Translation Skills ················ 121
聚焦价值引领 Focus on Values Education ················ 123

Unit Nine 产品说明书 Instructions ················ 124

热身练习 Warm-up Exercises ················ 125
文本功能及构成 Structure and Functions ················ 126
熟悉文本特征 Learn about Stylistic Features ················ 127
文本翻译实践 Do the Text Translation ················ 130
探索翻译技能 Explore Translation Skills ················ 132
巩固翻译技能 Enhance Translation Skills ················ 134
磨炼翻译技能 Sharpen Translation Skills ················ 135
拓展翻译技能 Broaden Translation Skills ················ 136
聚焦价值引领 Focus on Values Education ················ 139

Unit Ten 企业简介 Corporate Profile ················ 140

热身练习 Warm-up Exercises ················ 141
文本功能及构成 Structure and Functions ················ 142
熟悉文本特征 Learn about Stylistic Features ················ 143
文本翻译实践 Do the Text Translation ················ 147
探索翻译技能 Explore Translation Skills ················ 150
巩固翻译技能 Enhance Translation Skills ················ 154
磨炼翻译技能 Sharpen Translation Skills ················ 156
拓展翻译技能 Broaden Translation Skills ················ 158
聚焦价值引领 Focus on Values Education ················ 160

Unit Eleven 会展文本 MICE Texts ················ 162

热身练习 Warm-up Exercises ················ 163
文本功能及构成 Structure and Functions ················ 164
熟悉文本特征 Learn about Stylistic Features ················ 167

目 录

文本翻译实践 Do the Text Translation ·· 169
探索翻译技能 Explore Translation Skills ·· 171
巩固翻译技能 Enhance Translation Skills ·· 174
磨炼翻译技能 Sharpen Translation Skills ·· 175
拓展翻译技能 Broaden Translation Skills ·· 177
聚焦价值引领 Focus on Values Education ·· 179

Unit Twelve 商务报告 Business Report ································ 181

热身练习 Warm-up Exercises ·· 182
文本功能及构成 Structure and Functions ·· 183
熟悉文本特征 Learn about Stylistic Features ······································· 185
文本翻译实践 Do the Text Translation ·· 187
探索翻译技能 Explore Translation Skills ·· 190
巩固翻译技能 Enhance Translation Skills ·· 193
磨炼翻译技能 Sharpen Translation Skills ·· 195
拓展翻译技能 Broaden Translation Skills ·· 196
聚焦价值引领 Focus on Values Education ·· 198

Unit Thirteen 商务合同 Business Contract ··························· 199

热身练习 Warm-up Exercises ·· 200
文本功能及构成 Structure and Functions ·· 201
熟悉文本特征 Learn about Stylistic Features ······································· 202
文本翻译实践 Do the Text Translation ·· 208
探索翻译技能 Explore Translation Skills ·· 210
巩固翻译技能 Enhance Translation Skills ·· 213
磨炼翻译技能 Sharpen Translation Skills ·· 214
拓展翻译技能 Broaden Translation Skills ·· 215
聚焦价值引领 Focus on Values Education ·· 217

参考文献 ·· 218

Unit One
商务翻译基础
Essentials of Business Translation

 Learning Goals 学习目标

- 了解商务文本的文体特征；
- 掌握商务文本的翻译策略和方法；
- 翻译商务文本时，彰显博学笃志、精益求精的理念。

1. 找出与下列中文商务术语相对应的英文术语。

(1) 国际商务	A. instructions
(2) 求职信	B. certificate of experience
(3) 招聘广告	C. international business
(4) 工作经历证明	D. import and export business
(5) 公示语	E. job advertisement
(6) 会议日程	F. cover letter
(7) 企业简介	G. business trip
(8) 商品说明书	H. social letter
(9) 商务报告	I. corporate profile
(10) 销售信	J. certificate of origin
(11) 商务旅行	K. public sign
(12) 租赁合同	L. lease contract
(13) 社交信函	M. meeting agenda
(14) 原产地证书	N. sales letter
(15) 保险单	O. insurance policy
(16) 国际营销	P. international marketing
(17) 进出口业务	Q. business report
(18) 电子商务	R. electronic commerce

2. 将下面的工作经历证明译成中文。

Certificate of Experience

March 2, 2018

To Whom It May Concern,

  This is to certify that Miss Liu MeiYu was employed in our Advertising Department as graphic designer from January 2014 to the end of December 2017. During the time she faithfully attended to her duties. She left us of her own accord.

           From Tian Mei Advertising Co., Ltd.

           David Lin

           Personnel Manager

商务翻译概述
Overview of Business Translation

  随着全球经济一体化趋势的日益加快，全球贸易日趋融合，中国和世界各国的贸易往来日渐增多。作为国际经济交流和商务活动的语言工具，商务英语脱颖而出，成为一门新型的、综合性的专业学科。

  商务英语是英语的一种社会功能变体，是专门用途英语(English for Specific Purposes)中的一个分支。商务英语以普通英语为基础，具有普通英语的语言学特征。与此同时，商务英语亦是商务知识和英语的综合，因而具有其独特的语言特征。商务英语作为一种专门用途英语，还可以细分为广告英语、法律英语、航运英语、服装英语、包装英语、信函英语、经贸英语等多种功能变体英语。

  商务翻译是指在国际商务活动或国际商务场所中把商务文本转换成目的语的创作活动，具有很强的商务性和较强的针对性。商务文本可以指与国际贸易相关的进出口活动所涉及的各种书面文本，如外贸函电、进出口单证、商业广告、商务合同等，也可以泛指一切与商业活动直接或间接相关的实用文本，包括商务名片、公示语、证明文本，以及产品说明书、企业简介、旅游宣传文本、商务报告、会展文本等。

商务翻译涵盖经济、贸易、金融、管理、会展、物流、营销等诸多领域。要精准、规范地翻译商务文本，译者要具备以下素质。

1. 扎实的双语基本功

双语功底在此指译者的外语水平和中文水平，两者在翻译中同等重要，不可偏废。有翻译实践经验的人可能都对这样一句话感触颇深，即"不做翻译就不知道自己的外语不好"。其实，我们同样可以说："不做翻译就不知道自己的中文不好。"在翻译中对原文理解得很清楚，却苦于找不到恰当的中文表达，这样的情况也是屡见不鲜的。因此，一名合格的译者必须精通双语。商务英语翻译是一种涉及专业领域的翻译实践活动，扎实的中、英文语言功底就显得尤为重要。商务英语翻译工作者既要熟练掌握国际商务专业知识，又要熟练掌握商务英语/汉语的词汇、句式和篇章结构知识，确保译文精准流畅、严谨规范，促进跨文化交际的顺利进行。

2. 敏锐的跨文化意识

不同国家和地区的人由于文化背景、风俗习惯、人文地理、民族差异等方面不尽相同，对同一事物有时会做出不同的理解和反映，译者在进行商务翻译时要充分注意到这种差异，培养跨文化意识，防止文化差异带来的负面影响。比如，"白象"牌电池的品牌名不应该直译成"White Elephant"，因为White Elephant在英语中有"大而无用"的意思，如果将White Elephant用作电池品牌，产品在英语国家市场的销路可想而知。"芳芳"唇膏意在表现东方女性的柔美，而音译"Fang"在英语里却意为"毒牙"，因此，只能舍弃音译并另寻其他方法。总之，把产品销往国外之前，一定要事先了解对方市场的风俗文化，再把商品的品牌名称翻译成恰当的目的语，以提高产品知名度，并促进产品的销售。

3. 高度的职业责任感

高度的职业责任感是指译者必须意识到自己肩负的使命，要有兢兢业业、一丝不苟的态度，对不明白或不熟悉的内容要勤查、多问，不望文生义，不草率下笔。下面的一个实例可以说明一个没有职业责任感的译者会给企业和个人造成多么大的损失。据《中国消费者报》报道，北京某餐厅的卡式燃气炉燃气罐爆炸，在座的12名顾客均被不同程度烧伤，其中一个少女容貌严重被毁，双手致残，诉诸法律，索赔约160万元。而造成这一重大事故的原因之一是不负责任的译者将燃气炉上的英文说明"Never refill gas into empty can"(空罐绝不能再次充气)翻译成了"本罐用完后若无损坏可再次补充"。虽然悲剧的发生不只是因为一句错误的译文,但是每一个翻译工作者都应牢记:翻译工作责任重大,稍有不慎,就可能带来不良政治影响或巨大经济损失,绝不可草率行事。

总之,商务翻译涉及面很广,译者要通晓英、汉商务文本翻译技能,熟悉经济贸易、金融财会、企业管理等领域的业务知识,具备很高的跨文化交际能力及高度的职业责任感,从而精准、规范地翻译商务文本,为国家经济、贸易和文化事业的发展贡献力量。

熟悉文本特征
Learn about Stylistic Features

1. 词汇特征

除了某些商务文书(如合同等法律文件)会使用一些很正式甚至冷僻的词外,大部分商务文本用词规范、平实达意。

1) 使用专业词汇

商务涉及经济、贸易、金融、财务、会计、保险、广告等诸多领域,因此商务英语使用大量的相关词汇和行业术语。行业术语具有国际通用性,其意义精确,且不带有个人感情色彩,用于准确描述商务活动中的各个环节。

例1

> According to our customs stipulation, **Consular Invoice** is required for the imported goods, which should go with the **shipping documents** when negotiating with the bank.
> 根据我国海关规定,该进口货物需领事发票。该发票应在银行议付时同其他运输单据一起递交银行。

例2

> If you can accept US$4.50 per piece **FOB** Shenzhen, please send us your **Proforma Invoice**.
> 你方若能接受FOB深圳价每件4.5美元,请寄形式发票。

2) 名词化现象

名词化是指把句子中的动词或形容词转换为名词或名词短语,从而使名词或名词短语获得动词或形容词的意义而具有名词的语法功能。商务英语行文中的动词或形容词的名词化程度很高,且信息量集中,使整个文本显得客观、正式、严谨。

例3

> The **effectiveness** of the electronic computer lies in its great **speed** and **accuracy** in calculation.
> 电子计算机之所以效率高，是因为其运算速度快，而且计算准确。

例4

> A precondition for the success of the single market is that there must be **losers** as well as **winners**.
> 成功地实施单一大市场的前提是有的公司必有所得，有的公司必有所失。

3) 使用缩略语

在商务英语中，人们常用固定的缩略语来代替一些高频词汇和专有名词，并使这些缩略语成为交际双方所能接受的一种语言规范。缩略语通常由原单词的首字母组合而成，并且这些字母都是大写的形式。缩略语的使用能够有效提高商务活动的效率，节省交际双方的时间。常见的缩略语包括常用术语的缩略、国家/地区的简称及国际组织的简称等。例如，GDP (Gross Domestic Product，国内生产总值)、APEC (Asia-Pacific Economic Cooperation，亚太经济合作组织)、CBD (Central Business District，中心商务区)、CEO (Chief Executive Officer，首席执行官)等。

例5

> In order to effect shipment as required, please try to issue the relative **L/C** before the end of April.
> 为如期交货，请在4月底前开出相关信用证。

例6

> We will **T/T** the down payment before the establishment of the **L/C**.
> 开立信用证之前，我方将电汇定金。

2. 句式特征

1) 使用简单句、简短并列句和简短复合句

随着时代的发展及生活节奏的加快，商务文本(尤其是商务信函和广告文本)日趋口

语化和简单化，这一变化表现在语言结构上，就是简单句、简短并列句和简短复合句的频繁使用。

例7

> As requested in your letter of 21 June, we are enclosing our check for US$100.00.
> 按照你方6月21日来信的要求，随信附上100美元支票一张。

例8

> Awaiting your reaction, we remain with best regards.
> 等候回复，顺颂商祺。

2) 使用长句、复合句、并列复合句

商务合同、契约、单证等商务文本具有法律属性，所以其用语具有严密、准确的特点，这一特点表现在语言结构上，就是长句、复合句及并列复合句的大量使用。这类较复杂的句式也常见于商务报告。

例9

> This contract is made by and between the buyers and the sellers, whereby the buyers agree to buy and the sellers agree to sell the under-mentioned commodity according to the terms and conditions stipulated below.
> 本合同由买卖双方订立，因此买卖双方同意按照下面规定购买、销售以下商品。

例10

> Party A shall send technicians at Party B's expense to train Party B's personnel within 30 days after signing the contract.
> 甲方应于合同签订日后30天内委派技术员对乙方的工作人员进行培训，费用由乙方负责。

3. 语篇特征

商务英语语篇是指在国际商务活动过程中使用的各种正式与非正式文件，具有浓厚的行业特色，涵盖了范围广泛的对外经济贸易活动。根据篇章语言学，我们可以把经贸英语篇章分为三类：公文体、广告体和论说体。其中，商务信函、合同、经济法律文书、通知等表现为公文体形式；商品说明书、商业广告主要表现为广告体形式；商务报告、演讲等表现为论说体形式。当然，语篇是多种交际功能的集合体，商务英语语篇也不例外。例如，商业广告除具有呼唤功能和信息功能外，也往往具有表达功能，且具有一定的文采。因此，从事商务英语翻译的译者不仅要把握语篇的宏观结构，还要把握其微观结构，具备应对不同文体、不同语篇功能的能力。

1) 论说体特征

商务英语论说体多出现在为推广产品、服务所作的报告或演讲中。这类文体用词正式、严谨，开头和结尾常用一些套语，翻译时应把握其风格特点。

 例11

> Good morning, ladies and gentleman,
>
> I'm very glad to be here. As Ms. Evans said, the purpose of my presentation today is to familiarize you with the new EBP. As you probably know, EBP stands for Electronic Book Player. ABC Company put the original EBP on the market a year ago, but we have since developed an improved model which we believe will be a big seller in both China and the U.S. The new model is better than the old one in many ways. First of all, the old model had a rather small screen, so not much information could appear at one time. Hence, on the new model, we've made the screen much bigger. And...
>
> 女士们、先生们，早上好！
>
> 我很高兴能在这儿演讲。正如埃文思女士所说，今天我来这儿演讲的目的是使大家熟悉新的电子书播放器。我想大家可能已经知道，EBP就是英文"电子书播放器"的缩写。一年以前，我们在市场上推出了EBP，之后我们公司又开发出一种改良型机种。我们相信，这一新机种在中国和美国将会非常畅销。新型的EBP在许多方面都超过了旧机种。首先，旧型EBP画面太小，所以无法一次显示很多资讯。而在新机种中，我们把画面增大了许多。还有……

2) 广告体特征

英语广告用语简洁、生动、形象、富于感染力。汉语广告多用四字词组，讲究对称与平衡，语言精练、意味深长。一般来说，一则好的广告必须新颖、独特，能够引起公众的注意，同时必须让公众理解其传达的信息，进而接受广告中所宣传的产品或服务，最终根据自己的需要采取某种行动。因此，广告体的翻译尤其需要译者的创造性。

⬥ 例12

Fresh Up with Seven-Up.
君饮七喜，倍添精神。

⬥ 例13

To spread your wings in Asia, share our vantage point.
在亚洲展开您的双翅，同我们一起飞高望远。

3) 公文体特征

商务公文用词正式，句式结构复杂，遣词造句力求准确，语意严谨，逻辑性很强。在翻译商务公文时要尽量使译文在语义、风格上与原文保持一致，正确理解原文，然后用目的语准确地表达出来。

⬥ 例14

Within 30 days after the signing and coming into effect of this contract, the Buyer shall proceed to pay the price for the goods to the Seller by opening an irrevocable L/C for the full amount of US$ 30 000 in favor of the Seller through a bank at import point so that the Seller may draw the sum in due time.
买方须于本合同签字并生效后三十天内通过进口地银行开立以卖方为受益人的、不可撤销信用证以支付全部货款，计30 000美元，以便卖方及时提取款项。

⬥ 例15

In case no amicable settlement can be reached between the two parties, the case in dispute shall be submitted to arbitration which shall be held in the country/region where the defendant resides.
如双方达不成友好协议，争议可提交仲裁。仲裁在被诉方所在国/地区进行。

文本翻译实践
Do the Text Translation

下面通过两个典型任务来练习商务文本的翻译。

任务1. 根据提示将下面的英文广告译成中文。

American Express

Around the corner, around the world, we're round to help.

The time zone may change. The currency may change. The language may change. But one thing remains constant as you travel: the help of American Express at more than 1 200 Travel Services Offices in over 130 countries and regions. Even if you never need us, it's nice to know we're here to help.

Don't leave home without us!

Travel Services Offices of American Express Travel Related Company Inc., its subsidiaries and representatives.

1. 领会翻译提示

- 运用汉语修辞手法，调整句式结构；
- 原文总体客观、平实，译文应当适当渲染，增强可读性。

2. 写出汉语译文

任务2. 根据提示将下面的英文会展文本译成中文。

Welcome to the Asian Marketing Effectiveness Festival 2018. The event, which brings together clients, agencies, and media owners, is designed to recognize the outstanding collaborative efforts of brands and agencies in the Asia-Pacific region.

Over the past eight years, the awards have provided the industry with a platform to encourage great work and talent, thus elevating the standards of marketing in the region.

> We are proud to bring this important marketing event to Shanghai for the first time. The aim of the two-day festival is really to drive home the importance of ROI. What makes it different from other conferences is the international learning you will take away with you. In putting together the speaker line-up, we set out to identify the best creators and thinkers—crucially those that add value to consumers and businesses—and bring them to Shanghai in an effort to deliver a world-class event.

(资料来源：李富森，王耀强. 商务英语翻译(家电方向)[M]. 北京：中国商务出版社，2014.)

1. 领会翻译提示

- 准确翻译会展名称和行业术语；
- 原文中的非限制性定语从句可以单独译成一句，与译文其他部分衔接。

2. 写出汉语译文

_____
_____
_____
_____
_____
_____

接下来，我们结合上面所给的任务，具体探讨商务文本的翻译技能和方法。

1. 词汇层面上：译文精准，符合规范

商务英语在词汇使用上的最大特点是准确使用专业词汇。准确性是商务英语翻译的第一要求，没有准确性，原文的交际目的也就无法实现。在翻译中，需要根据文本的内容和使用语境辨别所译词语的含义是一般含义还是专业含义，从而给出精准译文。

例16

> Thank you for your fax of July 15, filing a claim with us for the loss and damage to the captioned goods.
>
> **译文**：贵方7月15日就标题货物短量和损坏提出索赔的传真已收到，深表感谢。
>
> **评析**：此句中贸易术语the loss and damage译为"短量和损坏"，the captioned goods译为"标题货物"，译文准确规范、简洁凝练。

例17

> The shipping documents for the consignment are now with us and we shall be glad if you will arrange to collect them.
>
> **译文**：货运单据现存我行，请安排前来赎单。
>
> **评析**：此句中贸易术语shipping documents和collect them分别译为"货运单据"和"赎单"，译文专业规范、准确地道。

2. 语句层面上：译文简洁、严密和庄重

高效、务实是现代商务活动的特征，商务英语文书译文也必须明白晓畅、简洁凝练，符合目的语的句式特点。

例18

> We hereby confirm having sold to you the following goods on the terms and conditions as specified below.
>
> **译文**：兹确认按下面的条款售予贵公司下述商品。
>
> **评析**：古体词hereby通常用作法律文件、合同、证明等正式文本的开头语，译成"特此""兹"，符合中文证明、协议的表达习惯，语气庄重而正式。

例19

> The buyers may, within 15 days after arrival of the goods at the destination, lodge a claim against the sellers for short weight being supported by Inspection Certificate issued by a reputable public surveyor.

> **译文**：货物抵达目的港15天内，买方可以凭享有信誉的公共检验员出示的检验证明向卖方提出短重索赔。
>
> **评析**：英文中表示时间的介词短语within 15 days after arrival of the goods at the destination放在the buyers may后面，译者将时间状语放在句首，译文符合汉语表达习惯，表意层次分明，时间关系清晰。

3. 语篇层面上：译文结构规范，功能完整

就商务英语语篇翻译而言，译者必须了解商务领域的行业规范和背景知识，熟悉商务运作各个环节所使用的成套术语和各类商务语篇的表述模式与结构，确保汉译文本在语篇结构模式和语篇交际功能方面最大限度地与原文保持一致。

例20

> Dear Sirs,
>
>   Thank you for your enquiry of 15 January and we are pleased to inform you that we have been given an option on M.V. Stella. This is a heavy lifter of 4 000 tons gross. The terms provisionally agreed are US$××per ton.
>
>   The ship can be ready for loading at Avonmouth at 40 days' definite notice around the end of March. Please fax if you wish us to conclude a voyage charter for you.
>
> Yours Sincerely,
John Smith
>
> **译文**：
>
> 尊敬的先生：
>
>   1月15日传真收悉。关于所询租船一事，我公司很高兴有权出租斯戴拉号轮。这是一艘4 000吨载运重件船，暂定条件为每吨××美元。
>
>   该轮接到肯定通知后40天内可于3月底左右到达埃文茅斯港准备装货。请电告是否要我方代贵公司签订租船合同。
>
> 约翰·史密斯敬呈
>
> **评析**：这是一封报价信，属于问题解决型语篇。作者首先提到对方信中咨询租船一事，然后提出解决方案，可以出租斯戴拉号载运重件船，暂定租金每吨××美元，并概述了货船到港装货时间。最后，作者询问是否代对方签订租船合同。译文语言简洁明了，语气诚挚有礼，在语气、语言和行文方式上与原文保持一致，能够表现出与原文相同的功能。

巩固翻译技能
Enhance Translation Skills

1. 将下面的中文企业简介译成英文。

> 作为一家全球领先的家电集团,海尔致力于为全球消费者享受美好的住居生活提供完美的解决方案。为了实现对全球消费者的承诺,海尔白电集团依托自己拥有的冰箱、空调、洗衣机、热水器、厨电产品等白色家电产品,不断为全球消费者创造最新的生活体验与美好的生活方式。

(资料来源:李富森,王耀强. 商务英语翻译(家电方向)[M]. 北京:中国商务出版社,2014. 有改动)

2. 将下面的英文会展文本译成中文。

> Driving growth through sustainability is fundamental for global, national, and business competitiveness in the 21st century. This year's program will focus on how to increase energy efficiency, lower carbon emissions, develop green technology, and rebuild basic infrastructure. It will also provide a systematic overview of key economic, industry, and technological developments that will reshape business and society for the foreseeable future.

1. 将下面的英文句子译成中文。

(1) We usually pick a candidate who interviews well and has good qualification and an impressive work record.

(2) Haier, the leading appliance maker in China, is well known in its home market for its innovative goods.

(3) Customers from various countries and regions are warmly welcome to establish and develop business contacts.

(4) This type of typewriter is portable and durable, economical and practical for both office and home use.

(5) E-commerce has become an important part of people's life and also a strong driver of China's market economy.

(6) Various machine parts can be washed very clean and will be as clean as new ones when they are treated by ultrasonics, no matter how dirty and irregularly shaped they may be.

(7) The parcel you post must be well packed. Inadequate packing can mean delay, damage, or loss at your expense.

(8) Please let us have your best quotation by tomorrow together with the appropriate time of shipment.

(9) The price of the commodity is $1 per unit, but if your order exceeds 1 million units, we will give you a 30% discount.

2. 将下面的会展文本译成中文。

> Our conference has lasted three days. It has achieved tremendous success. Eighteen scientists and scholars spoke at the conference. Many more aired their views freely at group discussions, which proceeded in a friendly and lively atmosphere. I benefited greatly by attending this conference.
>
> Science and technology are a kind of wealth created in common by all mankind. They must in turn serve needs of all people and work for the interest of world peace. Any nation or country must learn from the strong points of other nations or countries, and from their advanced science and technology. Science involves Herculean efforts and grueling toil. At the same time, it calls for creativeness and imagination. Let's join hands and explore the boundless universe in quest of the never-ending truth of science.
>
> Ladies and gentlemen, you have my best wishes for your still greater achievements in your career of science.
>
> Now, I declare the conference closed. Thank you.

拓展翻译技能
Broaden Translation Skills

1. 熟悉下面的商务词语并将它们用于自己的翻译作品。

(1) economic growth   经济增长

(2) full time employment   全职工作

(3) insurance rate   保险费率

(4) marketing agency   营销代理

(5) on a contract basis   以合同规定的方式

(6) economic globalization   经济全球化

(7) mutual benefit and win for all   互利共赢

(8) market-oriented   以市场为导向的

(9) defect in the education system   教育制度的不足之处

(10) cultural scenic sites   人文景观

(11) public facilities   公共设施

(12) cost factor   成本因素

(13) to issue a passport   签发护照

(14) binding contract   有约束力的协议

(15) direct financing   直接融资

(16) to establish business relationship   建立业务关系

(17) corporate charter   公司章程

(18) pricing strategy   定价策略

(19) fluctuation range   波动幅度

(20) competitive advantage   竞争优势

(21) on the average   平均水平

(22) fiscal problem   财政问题

(23) profitable business   有利可图的业务

(24) non-commercial account   非贸易账户

(25) free trade area   自由贸易区

(26) interpersonal relationships   人际关系

(27) package deal   一揽子交易

(28) environmentally sustainable development　环境的可持续发展

(29) share holding reform　股份制改革

(30) resource allocation　资源配置

2. 熟悉下面的商务语句并将它们用于自己的翻译作品。

(1) With a view to supporting your sales, we have specially prepared some samples of our new makes and are sending them to you, under separate cover, for your consideration.

为了协助你方的销售，我们已经特地准备了一些新产品的样品，正要另行邮寄给你方，以供你方考虑。

(2) Our insurance company is a state-owned enterprise enjoying high prestige and has agents in all main ports and regions of the world.

我们的保险公司是国有企业，享有很高的声誉，且在全世界各主要港口和地区都有代理。

(3) We take pleasure in enclosing the latest designs of our products, which are superior in quality and moderate in price, and sure to be saleable in your market.

我们很荣幸附上我们产品的新款式，该款式品质优良，价格适中，在你们市场上肯定会有销路的。

(4) Multinational bank's services include issuing letter of credit, buying and selling foreign exchange, issuing banker's acceptances, accepting Euro-currency deposits, and making Euro-currency loans.

跨国银行提供的服务包括开立信用证，买卖外汇，开立银行承兑，接受欧洲货币储存，以及提供欧洲货币贷款。

(5) You may have observed an upward tendency in the prices of raw materials, which has every indication of being maintained. Under the circumstances, we would like to remind you that a similar offer in the near future is mostly unlikely.

贵公司可能注意到了原材料价格的上涨趋势，种种迹象表明这种趋势将持续下去。在此情况下，我们想提醒你们，近期内不太可能再有相同的报盘。

(6) The developed countries are rich in skilled work force and capital resources, so they can concentrate on producing many technology-intensive products such as computers, aircraft, chips, and so on.

发达国家拥有大量的熟练劳动力和资本，所以能集中生产很多技术密集型的产品，比如计算机、飞机、芯片等。

(7) For the most part, negotiation comes down to the interaction between two sides with a common goal but divergent methods.

在大多数情况下,目的一致而方式各异的交易双方最终都要经过谈判来做成生意。

(8) We have learned from the Commercial Counselor's Office of your embassy in Beijing that you are importers of light industrial products.

我们从贵国驻北京大使馆商务参赞处获悉,你们是轻工业产品的进口商。

(9) It is not very difficult for buyers and sellers in domestic trade to get to know each other's financial status and other information, and payment is likely to be made in a straightforward manner.

在国内交易中,买卖双方了解对方的财务情况和其他有关信息并不难,支付可能以一种直接的形式进行。

(10) All services in business—such as gift wrapping, delivery, and credit—have a certain amount of costs associated with them, and these costs must be covered by higher prices.

商业中所有的服务,比如礼品包装、送货及赊账,都有相应的成本,而这些成本要靠较高的价格来弥补。

(11) We are sending you a sample book with a price list of our new products, the high quality of which, we trust, will induce you to place a trial order with us.

我们现在寄上一本样本及新产品的价目表,我们相信优良的品质一定会吸引你方试订我们的产品。

(12) In view of the large demand for this commodity, we would advise you to work fast and place an order with us as soon as possible.

由于该商品需求量大,我们建议你方早日做出决定,尽快向我们订货。

(13) The corporate charter authorizes the corporation to issue and sell shares of stock, or transfer ownership in the corporation, to enable the corporation to raise money.

公司章程授权公司发行和销售股票,转让公司所有权,以便为公司筹措资金。

(14) The recovery, in turn, bodes well for consumer spending, which has been lackluster in recent months.

反过来,经济复苏预示着最近几个月以来一直疲软的消费者支出将会上升。

(15) These factors drove sizable investment in wind, solar, and bio-fuels technology, as well as rapid development of renewable power projects.

这些因素促使大量投资都投向了风能、太阳能和生物燃料技术,推动了再生能源项目的发展。

(16) Employees think and act as entrepreneurs, leading to a greater degree of involvement. As the number of these entrepreneurial units increase, more leaders are needed to drive these enterprises. A strong entrepreneurial culture creates leaders from within.

员工像企业家一样思考和行动，这能够使得员工们更加投入。随着这种团队的数量增加，企业需要更多具有领导才干的人员。强大的企业文化可从企业内部创造出领导者。

研读党的二十大报告选段(汉英对照)，提升汉英文本翻译技能，培养国际视野、家国情怀和专业能力。

> 全党同志务必不忘初心、牢记使命，务必谦虚谨慎、艰苦奋斗，务必敢于斗争、善于斗争，坚定历史自信，增强历史主动，谱写新时代中国特色社会主义更加绚丽的华章。
>
> It is imperative that all of us in the Party never forget our original aspiration and founding mission, that we always stay modest, prudent, and hard-working, and that we have the courage and ability to carry on our fight. We must remain confident in our history, exhibit greater historical initiative, and write an even more magnificent chapter for socialism with Chinese characteristics in the new era.

(资料来源：http://cn.chinadaily.com.cn/a/202210/17/WS6350b1cfa310817f312f29d6.html)

请结合党的二十大报告选段(汉英对照)，撰写本单元学习体会。

Unit Two
商务名片
Business Card

Learning Goals 学习目标

- 了解名片的功能、构成及文体特征;
- 掌握名片的英汉翻译技能;
- 熟练翻译名片,译文准确流畅;
- 翻译名片时,彰显客观求实的精神,秉持推广企业的理念。

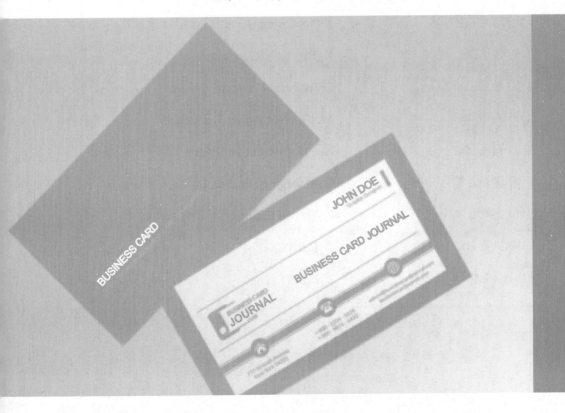

1. 找出与下列中文名片术语相对应的英文术语。

(1) 董事会	A. Engineering Department
(2) 行政管理部	B. Information Technology Department
(3) 工程部	C. R & D Department
(4) 研究开发部	D. Import & Export Department
(5) 采购部	E. Finance Department
(6) 进出口部	F. Public Relations Department
(7) 财务部	G. Human Resources Department
(8) 公关部	H. Board of Directors
(9) 人力资源部	I. Administration Department
(10) 信息技术部	J. Purchasing Department
(11) 首席执行官	K. Business Representative
(12) 注册会计师	L. Assistant Personnel Officer
(13) 人事助理	M. Certified Public Accountant
(14) 商务代表	N. Chief Executive Officer
(15) 总设计师	O. Managing Director
(16) 厨师长	P. General Editor
(17) 执行总裁	Q. Head Chef
(18) 总编辑	R. Chief Designer

2. 将下面的中文名片译成英文。

裕丰经济律师事务所 郭天明 法学硕士 律师 地址：北京市崇文区广渠门内大街80号 邮政编码：10×××× 电话：(010)5169×××× 传　真：(010)5169×××× 手机：1350116×××× 电子邮箱：guotianming@hotmail.com

文本功能及构成 Structure and Functions

商务名片是人们在商务活动、社交场合中进行自我介绍、信息传递的一种重要工具。随身携带名片，选择适当时机出示和交换名片是现代商务人士的必备礼仪。商务名片上通常印有企业徽标、注册商标、企业经营范围等内容。一般来说，大公司有统一的名片印刷格式，且名片用纸比较高档。商务名片属于"信息类"语篇，主要用于展示个人与其所代表的部门、公司和联系方式等，以便建立社交关系或处理业务。

名片没有统一的规格和固定的格式，但在我国，名片一般为9 厘米长、5 厘米宽的白色或黄色卡片。设计一张简洁而有效的名片是一种艺术，在合适的时候把名片递给合适的人也是一种本领，把名片背后的陌生人变成朋友更是对交际能力的一种考验。商务名片形式多样，但涵盖的文字信息基本相同，主要包括四部分内容：持有人姓名(name of the card holder)；职位或职称(position or title)；所在单位及部门名称(employment organization and sector)；联系方式(means of communication)，如通信地址、邮政编码、联系电话及传真、电子邮箱、网址等。

商务名片通常将持有人所在单位(或公司)标识和持有人姓名放在首位，这是为了突出其身份所属，同时树立公司形象；姓名和职位有时采用不同的字体，以便识别；然后是详细地址，英文地址按照从小到大的顺序列出公司所在的门牌号码、街道名称、市镇、国家/地区，汉语地址则与之相反；最后是联系方式，主要包括办公电话、传真、公司网址及电子邮箱等。

熟悉文本特征
Learn about Stylistic Features

1. 书写规范

商务名片的语言多由专有名词构成，因此英文名片上的每个实词首字母必须大写，有时名片持有人的姓名或企事业机构名称的所有字母都大写。下面给出了几个例子。

  人名：Mary Smith/MARY SMITH

  机构名称：Bank of China/BANK OF CHINA

  地址：23 Yaguan Road, Haihe Education Park, Tianjin P.R. China

2. 表达简练

因为名片空间有限，所以英文名片经常使用缩略语，以使其简洁明了。缩略语表现形式如下：

单个词语的缩写有时选取首字母并采取大写形式，如E(East)、S(South)、W(West)等；有时选取前两个或前三个字母进行缩写，如Fl.(floor)、Inc.(incorporated)、Tel.(telephone)、Apt.(apartment)等；有时只截取单词的辅音字母或者部分辅音字母进行缩写，如Rd.(road)、Rm.(room)、Bldg.(building)等。

两个或者三个单词构成的短语基本选取每个单词的首字母进行缩写，如H.P.(home phone)、E-mail(electronic mail)、CPA(certified public accountant)等。还有一些约定俗成的缩写形式，省略夹在其中的of、and等虚词，比如P.R.C.(the People's Republic of China)、MBA (Master of Business Administration)等。

3. 用词准确

为了宣传名片持有者及其代表的机构的形象，名片上的信息(如机构名称、部门名称、职务、职称、地址等内容)表达要准确无误。比如，中文"公司"一词在英文中有多种表达，如company、corporation、firm、services、holdings、agency 等。翻译企业名称时，必须了解这些词语的内涵，再根据公司的具体业务性质确定一个恰当的词语。如果选词不当，就会让他人对该企业的规模和组织形式产生误解。

文本翻译实践
Do the Text Translation

下面通过两个典型任务来练习商务名片的翻译。

任务1. 根据提示将下面的中文名片译成英文。

星光贸易有限公司

刘震　副总经理

地址：宁波市中山东路35号星光大厦B座702室　邮编：315000

电话：0574-8888××××　　　　　　　传真：0574-8888××××

手机：13500000000　　　　　　　　　邮箱：liuzhen@168.com

(资料来源：董晓波. 商务英语翻译[M]. 北京：对外经济贸易大学出版社，2011.)

1. 领会翻译提示

- 持有人姓名翻译；
- 单位及部门名称翻译；
- 职位、职称翻译；
- 联系方式翻译。

2. 写出英语译文

任务2. 根据提示将下面的英文名片译成中文。

```
            Texas Pipe and Supply Company
                    Andrew Edwards
                Marketing Department Manager
Address: 2330 Holmes Road, Houston    Zip Code: TX77051-××××
Tel: 001713-799××××                   Fax: 001713-799××××
E-mail: andrewed@texaspipe.com        Website: http://www.texaspipe.com
```

(资料来源：姜秋霞. 实用外事英语翻译[M]. 北京：商务印书馆，2015.)

1. 领会翻译提示

- 持有人姓名翻译；
- 单位及部门名称翻译；
- 职位、职称翻译；
- 联系方式翻译。

2. 写出汉语译文

____

接下来，我们结合上面所给的任务，具体探讨商务名片的翻译技能和方法。

探索翻译技能
Explore Translation Skills

1. 姓名翻译

无论是汉语姓名还是英语姓名，都包含两部分：姓氏和名字。由于两种文化在语言上存在差异，汉语姓名和英语姓名之间存在明显的不同：汉语姓名通常是姓在前，名在后，这体现了中国人强烈的家庭观念；而英文姓名则相反，一般是名在前，姓在后。考虑到中西方文化差异，一方面，将英语姓名译成汉语时，应尊重这一文化差异，把名放在前面，姓放在后面，名和姓之间用点隔开。例如，美国作家Helen Keller 应译成"海伦·凯勒"。另一方面，拼写汉语姓名时，姓氏在前，名字在后，复姓连写，双名连写，姓和名的首字母都大写。比如，将"王大鹏"译为"Wang Dapeng"，将"欧阳明"译为"Ouyang Ming"，等等。

在姓名的英汉翻译过程中，我们一般采用音译法，以实现指称意义上的信息对等。将英语人名译成汉语时，应尽量选择褒义或中性的词语，注意译名选字的约定俗成及性别差异。例如，英文姓名"Mary Smith"译为"玛丽·史密斯"，从"玛丽"二字可以推断出此人是一名女性。

按照"名从主人"的原则，如果一个人本身就取了英文名，应按照其英文名来翻译，而不能采取拼音翻译法。此外，有些名人的名字最初译成英文时曾受方言的影响，如孙中山 (SunYat-sen)，因沿用多年，已成定译，不宜更改。还有一些历史人物的名字，如孔子(Confucius)、孟子 (Mencius)等的英译文已经形成固定译法而广为流传，也不宜更改。由此可见，姓名的翻译重在查证。只有确定一个人没有固定的英文名或已沿用多年的译名后，才能采用音译法进行翻译。

2. 机构名称翻译

单位及部门名称属于专有名词范畴，通常词语排列及缩写形式相对固定，不应随意更改。在翻译过程中，译者须查阅相关资料，优先选择人们普遍接受的定译。比如，"中国农业银行"须译成"Agricultural Bank of China"，以免造成混乱。企业名称一般由企业注册地址、企业专名、企业生产对象或经营范围及企业的性质组成。企业注册地址按地名翻译的原则处理；根据实际情况，企业专名可音译，也可意译，音译时可按汉语拼音，也可按英语拼写方式来翻译；企业生产对象或经营范围须意译，两个并列成分一般用符号"&"连接起来，如"中国科学器材公司"译为"China Scientific Instruments & Materials Corporation"，但不宜在同一个名称里使用两个"&"符号，如"中国工艺品进出口公司"译为"China National Arts and Crafts Import & Export Corporation"。

值得注意的是,企业名称的表达形式要有所区别,不能把所有的公司都译成company,而应根据企业经营的性质进行英汉互译,做到用词规范、标准统一。具体用法如下:company(公司)一般指已经登记注册、具有法人资格的各种规模的公司,company常与limited连用(company limited,通常缩写为Co., Ltd.),译成"有限公司"。corporation一般是指"具有法人资格、能够独立经营的大型股份公司或大公司",常用于指总公司,比如China Mobile Communications Corporation(中国移动通信集团公司)。incorporated是美式英语,一般指股份有限公司,强调的是企业股份制性质,可缩写为Inc.,如Apple Inc. (苹果公司)。firm是指"两人以上合办企业或指从事商贸、经纪活动的单位",通常译为"商行、公司、事务所",如law firm(法律事务所)。group表示集团公司,如Wanda Group(万达集团)。holdings特指控股公司,即因持有其他公司的多数股权而对这些公司有控制权的公司,比如Mizuho Holdings(日本瑞惠控股公司)。

3. 部门名称翻译

现代企业按照职能设有多个部门,它们各司其职,分布于企业的生产、销售、服务及流通各个环节。在翻译过程中,译者应尽量找到英、汉两种语言中的对等表达,简洁明了地传递部门信息。

翻译企业部门名称和大学的系部名称时通常使用department。比如,将"人力资源部"译为"Human Resources Department",将"国际工程部"译为"International Engineering Department",将"商务英语系"译为"Business English Department",将"会计系"译为"Accounting Department",等等。

翻译政府机构、企事业单位的部门名称时,经常用到bureau(局)、section(处,科)等词语。比如,将"公安局"译为"Public Security Bureau",将"商务局"译为"Bureau of Commerce",将"财务处"译为"Finance Section",将"广告管理科"译为"Advertising Management Section",等等。

4. 职务/职称翻译

英汉职务/职称的翻译常常涉及两种语言的差异,而且和各自的社会制度、行业、习惯和历史背景有关。因此,英汉职称存在不对等的现象,翻译时经常出现难译或误译的情况。对于意思相近而功能不同的职位,译者要勤查工具书,还需要了解所属国家/地区的行政职务划分和职责功能,以确保译文符合规范、准确达意。

职务/职称中经常出现的"总"字(如总经理、总设计师、总编等)所对应的英文会有所不同。有的用chief进行翻译,如Chief Accountant(总会计师)、Chief Architect(总建筑师)、Chief Designer(总设计师)、Chief Engineer(总工程师)等，也可以用general进行翻译，如General Accountant(总会计师)、General Agent(总代理商)、General Dispatch Officer(总调度员)等，还可以用一些专门的词来翻译，如President(总裁)、Dean of General Affairs(总务长)、Head Clerk(总管)等。

译者翻译名片中的副职信息时，也要做到用词准确、规范。associate 表示专业技术职称的副职，如Associate Professor(副教授)、Associate Research Fellow(副研究员)等；deputy 一般指政府或企业部门的副职，如Deputy Manager(副经理)、Deputy Director (副主任)等；vice经常和president连用，表示国家副总统、国家副主席、企业副总裁、大学副校长等。需要注意的是，翻译英联邦国家的大学副校长时用Vice Chancellor。

5. 地址翻译

英语中普通名词构成的地名通常采用音译法，比如Madison Road(麦迪逊路)、Victorian Street(维多利亚大街)、Glasgow Road(格拉斯哥路)等。有时也采用意译法，如将Riverside Road译为"河边大道"，将West Park Avenue译为"西园大街"，等等。有些英文地名、路名已有了约定俗成的译名，在翻译时应采用现成的译法，以免产生误解。比如San Francisco(旧金山)、Los Angeles(洛杉矶)、Wall Street(华尔街)、Broadway (百老汇)等。

汉语地名分专名和通名：专名按照汉语拼音方案处理，首字母大写，不需要连接符；通名要按英文翻译，如广东省(Guangdong Province)、内蒙古自治区(Inner Mongolia Autonomous Region)、香港特别行政区(Hong Kong Special Administrative Region)等。专名和通名均为单音节的词，这时通名应视作专名的组成部分，先音译并与专名连写，后重复意译，分写，如蓟县 (Jixian County)、礼县 (Lixian County)等；专名为多音节，而通名为单音节的词，这时单音节的通名按专名处理，与专名连写，构成专名整体，如都江堰市(Dujiangyan City)、绥芬河市(Suifenhe City)等。

英文名片的地址采用由小到大的顺序，这与汉语的惯例正好相反。比如，"992 East Park Avenue, Rockford, IL61125, USA"译为"美国罗克福德市公园大道东路992号，邮编IL61125"；"北京市西城区金融大街3号"译为"3 Financial Street, Xicheng District, Beijing"。

中文邮政编码的通行写法是另起一行，前面标上"邮编 (Postal Code；Zip；P.C.)"两字，但英美各国的惯例却是将邮编直接写在州或城市的后面。比如：1120 Lincoln Street, Denver, CO 80203, USA (美国科罗拉多州丹佛市林肯街第1120号，邮编CO80203)；北京市东城区干面胡同51号，邮编100010 (51 Ganmian Alley, Dongcheng District, Beijing 100010, P.R. China)。

1. 将下面的中文名片译成英文。

山东外国语大学

章建军　教授

地址：中国青岛市香江路28号　　邮编：26××××

电话：(0532)8999×××× (办)　(0532)8999×××× (宅)

传真：(0532)8999××××　　　电子邮箱：zhangjj@sufs.edu.cn

2. 将下面的英文名片译成中文。

China Eastern Airlines Beijing Branch

Ma Chunfeng

General Manager

Address: 67 Wang Fujing Street Bejing, P.R. China

Tel: (010)46653××××　　Fax: (010)4032××××

E-mail: chfma@126.com

1. 将下面的中文名片译成英文。

清华大学出版社

贺×辉

外文编辑室　策划编辑

地址：北京市海淀区清华园街道双清路30号学研大厦　　邮编：10××××

电话：010-8266××××　　　传真：010-8265××××

手机：1300115××××　　　电子邮箱：lihui××@163.net

2. 将下面的英文名片译成中文。

Shanghai Dream-True Culture & Communication Co., Ltd.

Zhang Siyuan　General Manager

Address: 500 Hongqiao Road, Shanghai, China

Post Code: 20××××　　　Mobile: 1361234××××

Tel: 021-6543××××　　　Fax: 021-6543××××

Broaden Translation Skills 拓展翻译技能

1. 熟悉下面的部门名称并将它们用于自己的翻译作品。

    (1) Board of Directors　董事会

    (2) General Manager Office　总经理办公室

    (3) Headquarters　总部

    (4) Administration Department　行政管理部

    (5) Sales Department　销售部

    (6) Marketing Department　营销部

    (7) Business Office　营业部

    (8) After-sales Department　售后服务部

    (9) Accounting Department　财务部

    (10) Personnel Department　人事部

    (11) Advertising Department　广告部

    (12) Public Relations Department　公关部

    (13) Technology Department　技术部

    (14) Training Department　培训部

    (15) Customer Service Department　客户服务部

    (16) Reception Desk　接待处

    (17) Purchasing Department　采购部

    (18) Dispatch Department　发货部

    (19) Engineering Department　工程部

    (20) Import & Export Department　进出口部

2. 熟悉下面的职务/职称名称并将它们用于自己的翻译作品。

    (1) Chief Executive Officer　首席执行官

    (2) Executive Director　执行董事

    (3) Chief Operation Officer　首席运营官

    (4) Senior Customer Manager　高级客户经理

    (5) Marketing Manager　营销经理

    (6) Sales Representative　销售代表

    (7) Factory Director　厂长

(8) Head Nurse　护士长

(9) Technical Director　技术总监

(10) Financial Controller　财务总监

(11) Senior Accountant　高级会计师

(12) Purchasing Manager　采购经理

(13) Production Supervisor　生产主管

(14) Project Manager　项目经理

(15) Assistant to General Manager　总经理助理

(16) Assistant Personnel Officer　人事助理

(17) Associate Professor　副教授

(18) Associate Chief Physician　副主任医师

(19) Deputy Chief Engineer　副总工程师

(20) Director of Human Resources　人力资源总监

研读党的二十大报告选段(汉英对照)，提升汉英文本翻译技能，培养国际视野、家国情怀和专业能力。

> 十年来，我们经历了对党和人民事业具有重大现实意义和深远历史意义的三件大事：一是迎来中国共产党成立一百周年，二是中国特色社会主义进入新时代，三是完成脱贫攻坚、全面建成小康社会的历史任务，实现第一个百年奋斗目标。
>
> The past decade marked three major events of great immediate importance and profound historical significance for the cause of the Party and the people. We embraced the centenary of the Communist Party of China; we ushered in a new era of socialism with Chinese characteristics; and we eradicated absolute poverty and finished building a moderately prosperous society in all respects, thus completing the First Centenary Goal.

(资料来源：http://cn.chinadaily.com.cn/a/202210/17/WS6350b1cfa310817f312f29d6.html)

请结合党的二十大报告选段(汉英对照)，撰写本单元学习体会。

Unit Three

公示语
Public Sign

 Learning Goals 学习目标

- 了解公示语的功能、构成及文体特征；
- 掌握公示语的英汉翻译技能；
- 熟练翻译公示语，译文准确流畅；
- 翻译公示语时，彰显精准自然、引领价值的理念。

Unit Three 公示语 Public Sign

热身练习
Warm-up Exercises

1. 找出与下列中文公示语相对应的英文公示语。

(1) 教师休息室	A. No Food from Outside
(2) 迎宾酒家	B. Donate Blood to Save Lives
(3) 小心碰头	C. Admission by Ticket
(4) 一滴血，一片心，一份爱	D. Keep off the Lawn
(5) 凭票入内	E. Keep Our Earth Green
(6) 一起努力，海河更清澈	F. Yingbin Restaurant
(7) 小心地滑	G. Caution: Wet Floor
(8) 请勿践踏草坪	H. Faculty Lounge
(9) 请勿外带食品	I. Working Together for a Cleaner Haihe River
(10) 地球是我家，绿化靠大家	J. Mind Your Head
(11) 机场休息室	K. Check-in Area
(12) 办理登机区	L. Airport Lounge
(13) 消防通道	M. Close the Door after You
(14) 休闲广场	N. Entertainment Plaza
(15) 禁止停车	O. Business Center
(16) 随手关门	P. Fire Engine Access
(17) 商务中心	Q. No Parking
(18) 人行横道	R. Pedestrian Crossing

2. 将下列英文公示语译成中文。

(1) Set Down & Exit

(2) Ticket & Travel Center

(3) Restricted Height 3.3m

(4) Please Stand on the Right

(5) Handicapped Only

(6) This Is a Private Path No Admittance

(7) Short Stay

(8) Maintenance in Progress

(9) Post No Bill

(10) Beware of Pickpockets

文本功能及构成
Structure and Functions

公示语(public sign)是向特定人群传达特定信息以达到某种交际目的的文体。其应用范围非常广泛，涉及人们生活的各个方面，如街头路牌、广告牌、商店招牌、警示语、宣传语、公园景区提示语等。在我国，随着对外政治、经贸、文化交流活动的不断深入，越来越多的公共场所使用英文公示语，如机场、车站、宾馆、会展中心、旅游景点等，为来自世界各地的友人和商旅人士提供了方便。因此，译者必须提供恰当、得体的公示语译文。

公示语具有两个主要功能：信息传递功能和行为指令功能。信息传递功能是公示语

的基本功能，人们可以参照它所提供的信息做出某种选择。一般指示性公示语主要发挥信息传递功能。例如，当营业场所挂着"正在营业(Open)"的牌子时，顾客可以据此决定是否前去办理事务；相反，如果挂着的是"停止营业(Closed)"的牌子，顾客据此决定取消前去办理事务的打算。行为指令功能是指通过公示语向公众发布作为与不作为的指令。一般警示性公示语以行为指令功能为主。例如，"请勿大声喧哗(Keep Silence)"是向公众发出"保持安静"的指令，要求公众遵照执行。

依据英国翻译理论家彼得·纽马克(Peter Newmark)的文本类型论，公示语属于"提供信息+召唤行动"类语篇，具有发散性、公众性、空间有限和瞬间阅读等特点。因此，公示语的文本特点表现为形式短小精悍，传递的信息简洁明了，符合本地读者的接受习惯。如果公示语强调宣传功能，还要富有鼓动性和诉求性，促使读者按照公示语的要求说话、行事。

1. 使用名词短语

指示性公示语主要用来提供信息服务，为公众提示服务的内容。这类公示语往往使用名词结构或缩略语，从而直接、准确地显示特定信息。比如International Departure(国际出发)、Road Work(正在施工)、F&B(餐饮服务)、Caution: Pedestrians(注意行人)等。

2. 使用动词短语、祈使句

限制性公示语对公众提出限制、约束要求。为了将公众的注意力集中在所要求采取的行动上，这类英文公示语大多使用动名词或动词短语。将这类公示语译成汉语时，译者也要使用动词短语或祈使句式，使译文在语气、信息传递方面吻合原语。比如No Overtaking on Bridge(桥上严禁超车)、Please Do Not Disturb(请勿打扰)、Mind the Gap(注意站台缝隙)、Please Use Revolving Door(请走旋转门)等。

3. 文笔简练、措辞准确

英文公示语多省略冠词、代词、助动词等，仅使用实词、核心词汇，以便人们在最短的时间了解最准确、最直接的信息。从结构方面考虑，公示语经常使用短语或祈使句，体现简练清晰、一目了然的特征，比如Admission Free(免票入场)、Beverage Not Included(酒水另付)、Don't Drive When Tired(严禁疲劳驾驶)等。此外，英文公示语有时会借用一些简单的字母或数字来代替单词,如4 SALE(出售)、Merry X'mas(圣诞快乐)。

下面通过两个典型任务来练习公示语的翻译。

任务1. 根据提示将下列森林火灾提示语译成英文。

森林火灾

(1) 立即报警,说清起火方位、火场面积、燃烧的植被种类等。
(2) 身处火场,迅速躲到火已经烧过、杂草稀疏的平坦地带。
(3) 穿越火线时用衣物蒙住头部,逆风逃跑。
(4) 无路可逃时,用湿衣物掩盖外露皮肤。
(5) 不在林区吸烟、烧烤、上坟烧纸、点燃篝火、燃放鞭炮等。

(资料来源:陈娟.商务英语翻译实训教程[M].北京:电子工业出版社,2017.)

1. 领会翻译提示

- 注意汉、英句式结构的差异;
- 根据表达需要,使用英文定语从句,确保译文通顺、达意。

2. 写出英语译文

公示语 Public Sign | Unit Three

任务2. 根据提示将下列英文节水公示语译成中文。

> **PLEASE REUSE YOUR TOWELS**
>
> We invite you to join us to conserve water by using your towels more than once.
>
> In addition to decreasing water and energy consumption, you help us reduce the amount of detergent waste water that must be recycled within our community.
>
> Please hang the towels up if you wish to participate in the program—if not, simply leave them on the floor.
>
> We appreciate your help!

(资料来源：吕和发，蒋璐. 公示语翻译[M]. 北京：外文出版社，2011.)

1. 领会翻译提示

- 注意英、汉句式结构的差异；
- 根据表达需要，使用分译法，确保译文流畅，表意清晰。

2. 写出汉语译文

_____
_____
_____
_____
_____
_____
_____

接下来，我们结合上面所给的任务，具体探讨公示语的翻译技能和方法。

探索翻译技能
Explore Translation Skills

英、汉公示语在语言形式、文体特点和读者认知上有显著的差别。因此，译者在翻译公示语时，应分析英、汉公示语在语言和文化上的差异，把握目的语受众的心理文化特点，着眼于原语的意义和精神，不拘泥于原文的语言结构，而是采用灵活变通的翻译方法，产出简洁明了、准确达意的译文，实现原语文本和目的语文本在语言功能上的对等。

1. 遵从习惯，语言规范

公示语具有很强的归约性。受语言习惯的影响，很多公示语都已经约定俗成，不宜随意改动。翻译公示语时，译者应尽可能做到"入乡随俗"，采用目的语的习惯说法，实现目的语文本的预期功能。比如：前方修路，请慢驾驶(Road Work Ahead)；出租车招手停靠站(Taxi Stand)；自备零钞，不找零钱(Exact Fare Only)；Hard Hat Project(进入工地请戴安全帽)；For Display Only(陈列品不出售)；Handle at Your Own Risk(损坏后果自负)；等等。

2. 删繁就简，短小精悍

公示语要发挥其信息功能和指令功能，就必须做到语言精练、表意充分。在特定的语境中，公示语在翻译成另一种语言时，其语用含义比词语本身的含义更重要。此时，译者应删除烦琐部分，保留传达公示语功能的词汇，力求简洁清晰、意图明确。比如：汉语公示语"贵宾候车室"译为"Reserved Waiting Room"；"北京是我家，清洁靠大家"译为"Keep Our City Clean"；英语公示语"Close the Door behind You"译为"随手关门"；"Customer Care Is Our Top Priority"译为"顾客至上"。上述译文简练明了、表意充分，符合目的语表达习惯，实现了英、汉公示语的功能对等。

3. 程式化套译法

英文公示语的结构比较固定，程式化的套语运用广泛。因此，译者应根据具体情况，采用程式化套译法将中文公示语译成英文。下面列出了几个例子。

(1) "禁止做某事"套译为"No + 名词/动名词"的形式。比如：禁止掉头(No U-Turn)，禁止停车(No Parking)，禁止入内(No Admittance)，等等。

(2) "禁止/切勿做某事"套译为"Do Not +动词原形"的形式。比如：切勿打扰(Do Not Disturb)；警戒线，请勿跨越(Police Line, Do Not Cross)；等等。

(3) "×××专用"套用"名词+Only"的表达方式。比如：贵宾专用(VIP Only)，儿童专用(Children Only)，员工专用(Staff Only)，城市公交车专用车道(City Bus Only)，等等。

4. 反向翻译法

英、汉两种语言在逻辑思维方面存在差异。在翻译过程中，译者可以从反面将原文含义表达出来，使其符合目的语读者的文化认知习惯。比如：请勿将头伸出窗外(Keep Head Inside Vehicle)；无烟商场(Smoking Free Store)；工地危险，禁止入内(Danger, Building Site)；等等。

5. 创新翻译法

对于外国游客不容易理解的中文公示语，应根据英文的表达习惯遣词造句，采用创新译法，使译文语用得体，言简意赅，表意明确，取得预期效果。比如：司机一滴酒，亲人两行泪(Drink and Drive Cost Your Life)；桂林山水甲天下(East or West, Guilin Landscape Is Best)；携手合作，共创平安(Together We Can Prevent Crime)；文明行为，带来健康人生(Good Manners Make a Good Mind)；创一流服务，迎四海宾朋(First-class Services to All Guests)；等等。

1. 将下列英文公示语译成中文。

(1) In the interest of the public and the environment, please switch off your engine whilst stationary.

(2) Tickets are FREE from the admissions desk. Please ask a member of staff if you require assistance. Last Admission 5:30.

(3) Please consult the station map or a member of staff for location of cycle racks.

(4) Please DO NOT put other types of plastics in the bin.

(5) PLEASE DO NOT REMOVE ANY SUSPICIOUS DEVICES.

(6) Please have your ticket or boarding card ready for inspection.

(7) Please leave quietly as this is predominantly a residential area.

(8) Please offer this seat to elderly or disabled people or those carrying children.

2. 将下列中文公示语译成英文。

(1) 请重复使用毛巾

(2) 消防通道

(3) 您的安全，我们的天职

(4) 弯道危险

(5) 提高生活水平，迈向美好未来

(6) 凭此宣传品优惠15%

(7) 尊重知识，尊重人才

(8) 限速每小时48千米

1. 将下列英文公示语译成中文。

(1) Please use revolving door.

(2) Line up on the other side.

(3) Do not use elevator in case of fire.

(4) Children must be accompanied on escalator.

(5) This elevator does not lead to the downstairs toilet.

(6) The escalator is under repair. We apologize for any inconvenience caused.

(7) Flush after use.

(8) Caution: wet floor.

2. 将下列中文公示语译成英文。

(1) 温馨提示
(2) 安居工程
(3) 验票处
(4) 退票处
(5) 计时停车
(6) 加油站
(7) 市区
(8) 北门

拓展翻译技能
Broaden Translation Skills

熟悉下列五种公示语并将它们用于自己的翻译作品。

1. 标识性公示语

此类公示语主要用于提供信息，其功能在于指示服务的内容，广泛应用于旅游景点、商业场所、体育文化设施、卫生设施、涉外机构、街区名称等。大量使用名词结构或缩略语，能够直接、准确地显示特定信息，使人一看就明白。

例如：Information(问询服务)、Car Rental(租车服务)、Travel Service(旅游服务)、Take Away(外卖服务)、International Departure(国际出发)、Internet Café(网吧)、Drinking Water(饮用水)、Press Main Center(主新闻中心)、EXPRESS WAY(高速路)、Shopping Mall(购物商城)、P(停车场)、VIP Suite(贵宾候机室)、F&B(餐饮服务)等。

2. 提示性公示语

此类公示语仅起提示作用，广泛应用于公共设施、交通标志等，选择的词性及词组类型多样，使用能直接表达提示功能的词语即可。

例如：Reserved(预留席位)、Sterilized(已消毒)、Wet Paint(油漆未干)、Sold Out(已售完)、Explosive(易爆物品)、Blood Donation(献血处)、Turn Right(向右转弯)、Hold the Hand Rail(紧握扶手)、Roadwork(正在施工)、Handicapped Only(残疾人通道)、Please Pay Here(请在此交款)等。

3. 限制性公示语

此类公示语对相关公众的行为提出限制、约束要求，大量使用动词、动名词，语言直截了当，但语气委婉，不会使人感到强硬、粗暴。

例如：Give Way(让路)、Stand in Line(站队等候)、No Tipping(谢绝小费)、Keep Silence(保持安静)、Do Not Disturb(请勿打扰)、Keep Off the Grass(勿踏草坪)、Beware of Pedestrians(注意行人)等。

4. 强制性公示语

此类公示语要求相关公众必须采取或不得采取某种行动，因为如果公众不照办，可能造成危险后果，所以此类公示语语言直白、强硬，没有商量余地，常直接使用语气较强硬的动词，并且大量使用祈使句。

例如：No Through(禁止通行)、No Photography(严禁拍照)、Don't Drive When Tired(严禁疲劳驾驶)、No Dog Pooping(严禁狗便)、No Overtaking on Bridge(桥上严禁超车)、No Minors Allowed(儿童严禁入内)、Police Line: Do Not Pass(警戒线：勿超越)等。

5. 宣传性公示语

此类公示语对公众起到宣传、号召的作用，一般用句子表达。例如：

Let You Know the World 让您了解全世界
Better City, Better Life 城市，让生活更美好
Your Safety, My Responsibility 您的安全，我的责任
成功，源于对高品质的坚持 Success Comes from Unremitting Pursuit of Quality
尊重知识，尊重人才 Respect Knowledge and Talents
保护地球，我们唯一的家园 Let's Protect the Earth, Our Only Home
爱心接力代代传 Pass Love from Generation to Generation
撸起袖子加油干 Roll up Our Sleeves to Work Harder

研读党的二十大报告选段(汉英对照)，提升汉英文本翻译技能，培养国际视野、家国情怀和专业能力。

> 从现在起，中国共产党的中心任务就是团结带领全国各族人民全面建成社会主义现代化强国、实现第二个百年奋斗目标，以中国式现代化全面推进中华民族伟大复兴。
>
> From this day forward, the central task of the CPC will be to lead the Chinese people of all ethnic groups in a concerted effort to realize the Second Centenary Goal of building China into a great modern socialist country in all respects and to advance the rejuvenation of the Chinese nation on all fronts through a Chinese path to modernization.

(资料来源：http://cn.chinadaily.com.cn/a/202210/17/WS6350b1cfa310817f312f29d6.html)
请结合党的二十大报告选段(汉英对照)，撰写本单元学习体会。

Unit Four
求职文本
Job-hunting Texts

 Learning Goals 学习目标

- 了解求职文本的功能、构成及文体特征;
- 掌握求职文本的英汉翻译技能;
- 熟练翻译求职文本,译文准确流畅;
- 翻译求职文本时,彰显诚信为本的理念,力求展示个人风采。

求职文本 Unit Four
Job-hunting Texts

热身练习
Warm-up Exercises

1. 找出与下列中文求职文本术语相对应的英文术语。

(1) 个人资料	A. Research Program
(2) 荣誉及奖励	B. Educational Background
(3) 研究课题	C. Cover Letter
(4) 推荐人	D. Work Experience
(5) 求职目标	E. Certificate
(6) 简历	F. Personal Data
(7) 求职信	G. Internship Program
(8) 教育背景	H. Self-evaluation
(9) 工作经历	I. Job Objective
(10) 证书	J. Honors and Awards
(11) 特长及技能	K. College Diploma
(12) 社会活动	L. Résumé
(13) 实习经历	M. References
(14) 自我评价	N. Social Practice
(15) 大学文凭	O. Part-time Job
(16) 兼职工作	P. Specialties and Skills
(17) 婚姻状况	Q. Photography Competition
(18) 摄影比赛	R. Marital Status

47

2. 将下面的英文求职信功能句译成中文。

(1) I'm writing in reply to your advertisement in the Business Weekly for a part-time interpreter.

(2) I worked in a trading company as a part-time translator during my college years.

(3) I am skilled in almost all kinds of office machines and feel confident of my ability to fill the position of secretary.

(4) I am a person of responsibility, enthusiasm, and ability. I like challenges and I can quickly catch on to new procedures.

(5) I've enclosed a brief résumé. However, I will be very happy to provide you with further information about my abilities and experience in an interview with you.

(6) I should appreciate the privilege of an interview. I may be reached by letter at the address given above, or by telephone at 12345678.

求职文本
Job-hunting Texts

文本功能及构成 Structure and Functions

1. 简历

简历是用来介绍自己的个人资料、教育背景、工作经历、能力、业绩等情况的书面报告。对于求职者来说，简历无疑是求职的敲门砖。每个人都希望通过个性化的展示在招聘人员的心目中留下良好的印象，从而获得面试机会。简历应力求突出重点，语言简洁，篇幅适宜。简历通常包括以下六部分。

1) 个人资料(Personal Data)

个人资料部分主要包括姓名(Name)、性别(Gender)、国籍(Nationality)、地址(Address)、移动电话(Mobile Phone)、出生日期(Date of Birth)、出生地(Place of Birth)、健康状况(Health)等信息。

2) 求职目标(Job Objective)

这部分列明求职目标/岗位，让企事业单位工作人员明确你的求职方向和岗位，以便安排接下来的面试。

3) 教育背景(Educational Background)

简历的教育背景部分一般按逆时间顺序表述，从距现在最近的求学经历写起，主要包括大学教育和高中教育经历，列明求学起止时间、院校名称、取得的学历及学位等信息。

4) 工作经历(Work Experience/History)

工作经历一般按逆时间顺序表述，从距现在最近的工作经历写起，列明起止时间、工作岗位、工作职责和工作业绩等信息。

5) 特长及技能(Specialties and Skills)

这部分简要描述求职者的专业能力、技能特长，列明持有的资格证书、荣誉证书、计算机等级证书、外语水平证书等信息。

6) 自我评价(Self-evaluation)

这部分简要描述求职者的个人优势、性格特点、团队精神、工作态度、职业目标及职场竞争力等信息。

求职者根据简历的版式和应聘公司的要求，有针对性地选取以上各项内容，力求撰写内容精当、重点突出的简历，以争取面试的机会。

2. 求职信

求职信是指为了谋求一个工作职位而推介自己的一种常用的商务性信函，主要作用是向招聘者提供求职者的有关信息，使招聘者了解求职者的基本情况以便确定该求职者是否满足招聘者的需求。求职信类似于自我推荐信，是一种比较正式的文体，它不像推荐信那样严肃，但要求格式规范。

求职信的语气应恳切、礼貌，因此翻译时应该把这种态度与感情表达出来。同时，求职信篇幅切忌过长，翻译句子时也不应该啰唆，要保证表述能够吸引人，简短清晰。

求职信主要包括以下几部分。

1) 表明写信目的

求职信开头应表明写信目的——申请岗位，并且交代职位信息来源，这样求职信显得自然、顺畅。

2) 介绍个人经历

应聘者简要描述自己的教育背景——所学专业课程及掌握的职业技能，然后描述和应聘职位相关的工作经验和业绩；应届毕业生无全职工作经验，可以简述兼职工作经历、社会实践活动来突出你的优点。

3) 提出获职打算

应聘者针对公司的需求和目标提出自己的认识，表示应聘成功会努力工作，出色完成任务，为公司发展做出贡献。

4) 致谢盼复

求职信的结尾一般要向收信人致谢，感谢对方花时间阅读你的求职材料，同时表达与之面谈的期盼之情。

熟悉文本特征
Learn about Stylistic Features

1. 简历

1) 使用缩略语

因简历篇幅有限，翻译过程中经常使用缩略语，力求简单明了。例如："文学学士"译为"B.A.(Bachelor of Arts)"，"工商管理硕士"译为"MBA(Master of Business Administration)"，"注册会计师"译为"CPA(Certified Public Accountant)"，等。然而，有些专门机构和术语的简称流行面不广，最好不用简称，比如PMP—Production Management Plan(生产管理计划)。

2) 使用简单句式

简历语言要简明得体，以便读者准确把握主旨。通过名词短语、动词短语或形容词短语表达完整语义。比如：Excellent Editor Award of Campus English Radio Station(校园英语广播站优秀编辑奖)；Enjoy working with other people(愿意与人共事)；Proficient in written and spoken English(熟练运用英语口语和书面语)；等等。通过使用行为动词来描述应聘者做过什么和能做什么。比如：Developed and conducted on-site seminars(发起并主持了现场研讨会)；Arrange major project activities and manage changes in project process(安排大型项目活动并协调项目过程中的变动)；等等。

2. 求职信

1) 语句简洁明了

求职信是目的性极强的应用文体，语言要简洁明了，避免使用太多的术语和过于复杂的句子。求职信应开门见山，直接表达目的，说明你在哪家媒体看到应聘广告及所要应聘的职位。比如，I am writing this letter to apply for the post of Financial Manager advertised in the Business Weekly on July 4。在说明教育背景时，也应该言简意赅，比如，When I was at university, I received specialized training in logistics management。

2) 语气不卑不亢

英文求职信中，求职者须避免自我吹嘘，不要写自己不具备的能力。但是，过分自谦又令人怀疑其才学和能力。因此，求职者要使用准确达意的语言，以获得用人单位的认同。比如，I am confident that my expertise and referees will show you that I can fulfill the particular requirements of your secretarial position。通过这样的语句，求职者既给人一种自信感，又无自夸之嫌。

下面通过两个典型任务来练习求职文本的翻译。

任务1. 根据提示将下面的英文简历译成中文。

Résumé

Name: Li Yong　　　　Gender: Male

Mobile Phone: 1398032××××　　E-mail: globalli@yahoo.com.

Address: TCL Communications Apparatus Co., Ltd., South Eling Road, Huizhou

Objective: Electronics Engineer

Education Background

2007.9 – 2011.6 B.S. in Electronics, Shanghai Jiaotong University

2002.9 – 2007.6 Shanghai No. 112 Middle School

Work Experience

2022.1 – Present Senior Engineer at TCL Communications Apparatus Co., Ltd., Huizhou

In charge of the development of electronic telephone equipment

2016.7 – 2021.12 Engineer at Guangzhou Telecommunication Bureau

Responsible for assembling movable telephone exchanges

2011.7 – 2016.5 Assistant Engineer at Shanghai Airplane Manufacturing Plant

Assisted in designing electronic components of the flight deck

Technical Qualifications

Assistant Engineer Certificate, 2013

Engineer Certificate, 2018

Membership

Director of Guangdong Branch, China Institute of Communication

Certificates and Skills

Language: CET-6 & proficient in listening and speaking

Computer: Certification of Intermediate-level Skills of Computer Operation of Shanghai

Self-appraisal

Enjoying working with others

Responsible and reliable

Willing to be challenged with responsible work

(资料来源：房玉靖，马国志. 商务英语写作[M]. 2版. 北京：清华大学出版社，2021.)

1. 领会翻译提示

- 使用动词短语翻译工作职责和自我评价；
- 使用动词短语翻译专业技能。

2. 写出汉语译文

任务2. 根据提示将下面的英文求职信译成中文。

Dear Mr. Xu,

In response to your advertisement in China Daily on June 15, I wish to apply for the position of sales assistant.

Majoring in International Marketing, I will be graduating from Tianjin College of Commerce at the end of this June. During my past years of study at college, I have grasped the principal knowledge of my major and skills of practice. Not only have I passed CET-6, but more importantly I can communicate with others freely in English. My ability to write English is out of question. Therefore, I believe you will find me well qualified for the job.

I am really interested in learning business practice, and I am also a diligent worker and a fast learner. If given a chance, I am sure I can prove my worth in your company.

I will be available during the weekdays in the morning for any interviews you may want to give. Enclosed is my résumé, and I'm hoping for your immediate reply.

Yours Sincerely,
Zhang Ming

(资料来源：房玉靖，马国志. 商务英语写作[M]. 2版. 北京：清华大学出版社，2021.)

1. 领会翻译提示

- 根据表达需要,将介词短语in response to...译成并列分句;
- 采用灵活手段翻译套语I will be available during... for...。

2. 写出汉语译文

接下来,我们结合上面所给的任务,具体探讨求职文本的翻译技能和方法。

1. 简历

中、英文简历在行文顺序和句式结构上有很大差异。因此,译者要遵循目的语表达习惯,灵活调整原文语句结构,从而写出表意准确完整、语言简洁流畅的译文。

1) 求职目标翻译

将求职目标译成英文时通常使用名词短语或不定式短语,使其符合英文简历的表达习惯。

例1

> 求职目标
> 谋求一个具有挑战性的职位——销售经理
> Job Objective
> To obtain a challenging position as a sales manager

例2

求职目标
公关经理
Job Objective
Public Relations Manager

2) 工作职责翻译

简历中用英文描述过去的工作经历时，使用过去时态；描述目前的工作经历时，用一般现在时。

例3

管理海外市场业务(过去的工作职责)
Managed overseas market business

例4

为不同企业开发国际商务课程(当前的工作职责)
Develop international business classes for different enterprises

3) 特长及技能翻译

将求职者的技能及特长译成英文时通常使用动词短语、形容词短语，力求使译文简洁明了，表意清晰。

例5

会计技能：
通晓一般会计程序
Accounting Skills:
Have a strong knowledge of general accounting procedures

例6

> 计算机技能：
> 熟练使用MS FrontPage、Win95/NT、Sun、JavaBeans、HTML、JavaScript
> Computer Skills:
> Proficient in use of MS FrontPage, Win95/NT, Sun, JavaBeans, HTML, JavaScript

4) 个人评价翻译

将简历中的个人评价翻译成英文时，可以使用名词短语、形容词短语、动词短语等结构，确保语言流畅、简洁明了。

例7

> 能够独立工作，思想成熟，应变能力强
> Able to work independently, mature, and resourceful

例8

> 愿意在压力下工作，并具备领导素质
> Willing to work under pressure with leadership quality

例9

> 有协调能力及团队合作精神
> Have coordination skills and team spirit

2. 求职信

求职信是针对不同用人单位的一种书面自我介绍，首、尾部分的翻译应注意礼貌用词。中、英文求职信在语句结构和措辞上存在很大差异。因此，译者应灵活调整原文语序结构，使译文准确流畅、语气诚恳，获取读信人的赞赏和认可。

1) 礼貌用词，语气诚恳

求职信的语气应恳切、礼貌，传达求职者的真诚、有礼。因此，翻译时应该把这种态度与感情表达出来，从而打动企事业单位招聘人员，获得面试的机会。

例10

I am writing to enquire whether you have a vacancy for me in your organization.
写信询问贵单位是否有适合本人的职位空缺。

例11

I shall be obliged if you will give me a personal interview at your convenience.
如您方便时给予面试机会,我将不胜感激。

例12

I hope you will consider my application and I look forward to meeting you.
希望您考虑我的申请。盼望与您面谈。

2) 使用套语,准确规范

在求职信中,求职者表达应聘职位的意愿,并试图通过阐述自己的能力和特质,得到招聘企业的认可。因此,翻译求职信时,要使用目的明确、语言简练的套语,体现求职者的真诚意愿和良好的职业能力和素养,以争取面试的机会。

例13

I wish to apply for the post of flight attendant, which was advertised in Beijing Daily on November 10, 2022.
看到贵公司2022年11月10日在《北京日报》上刊登的广告,本人拟申请乘务员职位。

例14

I have received a good education, and I have business knowledge and know the sales techniques.
本人受过良好的教育,不但具有商业知识,而且熟悉销售技巧。

例15

I have learned from www.chinaHR.com that there is a vacancy in your firm, and I wish to apply for the post of Executive Secretary.

从中华英才网上得知贵公司有职位空缺,本人拟申请行政秘书职位。

例16

Enclosed please find my résumé, a copy of college diploma, and a letter of recommendation.

随函附上本人简历、大学文凭一份及推荐信一封。

3) 英语长句,拆分处理

在英文求职信中,求职者时常使用一些结构复杂的句子描述自己的教育经历、工作经历,以凸显自己的工作业绩和竞争优势。将英文长句译成中文时,要理清内容脉络,拆分原文结构,写出用词准确、层次清楚、简洁明了的译文,并使其符合目的语的表达习惯。

例17

I am to complete the four-year commercial courses and graduate this July from Beijing Technology and Business University. During my summer vacation, I was employed in the accounting department of a chemical company.

今年7月本人将读完四年的商科课程并从北京工商大学毕业。在暑假期间,我曾受雇于一家化学公司的会计部。

例18

I am thirty-six years of age, and have had ten years' experience in my present job, which I am leaving to better myself.

本人今年36岁,在目前的工作岗位已有十年工作经验,现准备离开此职位,以谋求更大的发展。

例19

My strong service orientation and bias for action would serve your company well in response to the needs and concerns of your clients.

我强烈的服务意识和行动力将能很好地为公司服务,以满足贵公司客户的要求。

例20

As you can see from the enclosed résumé, my reputation as a creative, innovative contributor is well supported by 22 registered patents and an additional 18 patent disclosures.

正如您在简历中看到的一样,我拥有22个注册专利和另外18个专利披露,这足以证明我是一个有创造力和创新精神的人。

1. 将下面的中文简历译成英文。

> 詹帆
> 联系电话:1520144××××　邮箱:zfan92@163.com
> 通信地址:北京海淀区清华东路35号北京林业大学12号楼205
> **求职目标**
> 在银行业获取一个初级职位
> **教育背景**
> 2015.9 — 2019.6　上海对外经贸大学　法学文学士
> **工作经验**
> 2017.7 — 2017.8　上海博物馆　志愿解说员
> 2016.9 — 2017.6　英语俱乐部　副社长
> 2016.3 — 2016.12　上海对外经贸大学学生创业中心管理服务中心市场部　助理

获奖情况

国家奖学金(2017—2018学年)、校优秀学生奖学金(2016—2017学年)

专业技能

语言水平：中级口译证书　英语六级(525)

计算机水平：熟练掌握办公软件操作

2. 将下面的英文求职信译成中文。

Dear Mr. Zhang,

　　I would like to apply for the position of Hotel Guestroom Manager offered by your company in the advertisement published in Beijing Evening News.

　　Enclosed is my résumé as per your requirements. I have been working in Henry Hotel since my graduation from Tianjin Foreign Studies University. Six years of dedication, starting from the basic tasks, such as the work at reception, guestroom, and food and beverages etc., has enabled me to accumulate a wealth of hotel management experience. At present, I am the manager of Henry Hotel.

　　I am modest, gentle, enthusiastic, and meticulous in my work. The reason for my present application to your company is that I am longing to meet challenges to take part in the management of a reputable large hotel group.

　　Should you give me a notice two or three days ahead, I will be ready to accept your interview on time.

　　　　　　　　　　　　　　　　　　　　　　Sincerely Yours,
　　　　　　　　　　　　　　　　　　　　　　Zhao Ming

1. 将下面的中文简历译成英文。

刘晶

联系电话：1368110×××× 邮箱：liuj2001@126.com

通信地址：天津商业大学学生宿舍9楼108室

求职目标

成为一名助理会计

教育背景

2019—2023 天津商业大学 会计专业管理学学士

主修课程：

会计原理、财务管理、簿记原理、成本分析、成本会计、经济数学、商业统计、计算机数据处理、西方金融系统、商业英语

工作经历

2021.7—2022.8 兼职销售员 天津好运家电有限公司

获得了产品和价格方面的知识

获奖情况

天津商业大学优秀学生(2020—2021)

证书和技能

英语：通过大学英语六级(550分)

计算机：通过全国计算机等级考试(二级)

自我评价

自信、细心、诚实

2. 将下面的中文求职信译成英文。

> 尊敬的先生：
>   看到贵公司在智联招聘网站刊登的广告，我拟应聘销售经理一职。敬请予以考虑。
>   我于2018年6月毕业于上海大学。过去五年，我在思科系统网络技术有限公司上海分公司从事销售工作。到目前为止，我担任该公司政府公共事业部销售经理已有一年半时间。
>   我之所以想换工作，是因为感觉目前工作的发展空间不大。我认为自己凭自身能力和所受训练，理应获得更好的职位。但我目前的工作岗位似乎无多大发展前途。
>   如您愿意接见本人以进一步了解我的能力，我将随时与您面谈。
>
>   李杰敬呈

拓展翻译技能
Broaden Translation Skills

1. 熟悉下面的求职文本表达语并将它们用于自己的翻译作品。

(1) Fluent in spoken and written English.
熟练使用英语口语和书面语。

(2) Skilled in use of Microsoft Office.
擅长使用微软办公软件。

(3) Follow up the market change and prepare monthly analytical market report.

紧跟市场动向并编制月度市场分析报告。

(4) Identify new business opportunities with West China.

探索中国西部的商机。

(5) Submit monthly revenue report to the management on time.

按时向管理人员提交月度营业利润报告。

(6) Maintained daily reports involving return guests, corporate accounts, and suite rentals.

完成每日报告，涉及回头客、公司账款及套房出租事项。

(7) Tracked best-selling novels and made recommendations to customers.

追踪畅销小说并为客户推荐。

(8) Highly skilled in problem solving and able to work under pressure.

非常擅长解决问题且具备抗压能力。

(9) Team player, able to work independently, self-motivated, and skilled at communication.

具有团队合作精神、独立工作能力、上进心及良好的沟通技巧。

(10) Aggressive, independent, and able to work under a dynamic environment.

积极进取，独立性强，能够在动态环境下工作。

2. 熟悉下面的求职文本功能句并将它们用于自己的翻译作品。

(1) My solid academic background will meet your general entrance requirements for graduate study.

我坚实的教育背景符合您在入职条件方面对学历的要求。

(2) I feel I have the necessary skills and interest to be an excellent contributor to your organization.

我感觉我具备了服务贵组织所必需的技能并很乐意成为一名优秀的员工。

(3) My résumé is enclosed for your reference.

随函附上简历，供您参考。

(4) I would like the chance to put my energy, drive, and enthusiasm to work for a company such as yours.

我很乐意把我的精力、动力和激情都投入贵公司的工作中。

(5) I am a conscientious person who works hard and pays attention to details.

我是一个认真、负责且注重细节的人。

(6) I'm flexible, quick to pick up new skills, and eager to learn from others.

我的头脑灵活，容易学会新技能并渴望向他人学习。

(7) I have extensive experience in the following specialty areas.

我在以下专业领域经验丰富。

(8) I might make efforts to your new product development.

我可以为你们的新产品开发工作而努力。

(9) I would appreciate your time in reviewing my enclosed résumé.

非常感谢您利用宝贵时间看我随信附上的简历。

(10) I would welcome an opportunity to meet you for a personal interview.

我希望能有机会进行面试。

研读党的二十大报告选段(汉英对照)，提升汉英文本翻译技能，培养国际视野、家国情怀和专业能力。

> 中国式现代化的本质要求是：坚持中国共产党领导，坚持中国特色社会主义，实现高质量发展，发展全过程人民民主，丰富人民精神世界，实现全体人民共同富裕，促进人与自然和谐共生，推动构建人类命运共同体，创造人类文明新形态。
>
> The essential requirements of Chinese modernization are as follows: upholding the leadership of the Communist Party of China and socialism with Chinese characteristics, pursuing high-quality development, developing whole-process people's democracy, enriching the people's cultural lives, achieving common prosperity for all, promoting harmony between humanity and nature, building a human community with a shared future, and creating a new form of human advancement.

(资料来源：http://cn.chinadaily.com.cn/a/202210/17/WS6350b1cfa310817f312f29d6.html)

请结合党的二十大报告选段(汉英对照)，撰写本单元学习体会。

Unit Five
证明文本
Certificate

 Learning Goals 学习目标

- 了解证明文本的功能、构成及文体特征；
- 掌握证明文本的英汉翻译技能；
- 熟练翻译证明文本，译文准确流畅；
- 翻译证明文本时，彰显客观公正和精益求精的理念。

1. 找出与下列中文证明文本术语相对应的英文术语。

(1) 报关员资格证书	A. tour guide certificate
(2) 毕业证书	B. chemical skills certificate
(3) 导游资格证书	C. accounting certificate
(4) 股份证书	D. graduation certificate
(5) 国家司法考试证书	E. second-level certificate for national computer
(6) 化学技能证书	F. business English certificate
(7) 会计证	G. medical certificate
(8) 普通话等级证书	H. certificate of customs specialist
(9) 全国计算机二级证书	I. national judicial examination certificate
(10) 商务英语证书	J. securities business qualification certificate
(11) 委托书	K. technician certificate
(12) 体检证明	L. national mandarin test
(13) 证券从业资格证书	M. certificate of chartered financial analyst
(14) 注册金融分析师证书	N. share certificate
(15) 技工证	O. certificate of appointment
(16) 生活补助证书	P. marriage certificate
(17) 结婚证书	Q. attorney's certificate
(18) 律师资格证书	R. living aid certificate

2. 将下面的英文证明文本译成中文。

> **Certificate of Merit**
>
> This is to certify that Mr. Yang Lei has won the title of Rising Star for his outstanding work in the emulation campaign of the year of 2022.
>
> Leading Import and Export Corporation
>
> Date: May 5, 2022

1. 证书

证书是政府机关、教育机构、企事业单位出具的文件，证明相关人员具备某种教育背景、技能特长、执业资格、权利与义务等，一般须加盖单位印章。证书在文体上不是书信，而是公文，具有较强的法律效力。证书通常由名称、日期、编码、照片、正文、出具单位、署名、签章等部分组成。常见的证书有毕业证书、学位证书、结婚证书、获奖证书、职业资格证书、技能证书、公证书等。

1) 名称

证书名称写在第一行的正中间，需要写明证书的具体类别信息，如毕业证书

(Graduation Certificate)、奖学金证书(Certificate of Scholarship)、公证书(Notarial Certificate)、结婚证书(Marriage Certificate)、资格证书(Qualification Certificate)等。

2) 正文

作为证书的核心部分，正文具体说明持证人的身份、学历、技能、资格、婚姻状况或健康状况等信息。英文证书的功能句式有"This is to certify that..."" It is hereby to certify that..."，译成汉语为"兹证明……""特此证明……"。

3) 署名及签章

作为政府机关、教育机构、企事业单位出具的文件，证书要在结尾处署签发机构的名称，并加盖机构公章，以彰显证书的权威性和严肃性。

2. 证明

证明是国家机关、社会团体、企事业单位为证明有关人员的身份、经历或其与某事件的关系而出具的函件，用真实、可靠的材料证明某人或某事的表现、特征。常用的证明信有出生证明、身份证明、在职证明、学历证明、健康证明、病假证明、存款证明等。

证明类文书通常体现为信件格式，但比一般书信要简单得多，由标题、称谓、正文、署名或签章等构成。

1) 标题

标题"Certificate/Testimonial"写在公文纸第一行的正中间，也可以具体写明该证明是哪方面的证明，如学历成绩证明(Schooling Record Certificate)、健康证明(Health Certificate)、存款证明(Deposit Certificate)等。

2) 称谓

证明信不必写收信人的姓名、地址，称谓多用"Dear Sirs (尊敬的先生)"或"To Whom It May Concern (敬启者)"表示。

3) 正文

正文是证明信的核心部分。根据不同的内容，篇幅长短不一。通常使用较正式的语言，多以"This is to certify that..." 或"It is hereby to certify that..."开头，相当于汉语证明中的"兹证明……""特此证明"。

4) 署名或签章

一般情况下，证明信结尾无结束敬语。证明信通常是国家机关、社会团体或工作单位出具的。因此，结尾要署机关、单位的名称，并加盖公章。署名位于正文右下角。

1. 证书

证书是能力、资格、权利、责任的有效证明，因而在语言表述上具有自身的特点。一方面，证书具有一定的法律效力，因而用语正式、措辞规范、遣词恰当、言简意赅。证书中经常用到of his own will(出于自愿)、whereof(关于)、confer/grant(授予)、hereby(兹)、It's suggested that...(建议……)等规范词语。

另一方面，证书中含有自身的套语。比如，英语证书中常用的"This is to certify..."或"We the undersigned(署名者) hereby certify that..."，在汉语证书中要译为"兹证明""特此证明"；汉语证书中的"同意授予……资格"，在英语中表述为"be admitted to..."或"The trusted have conferred upon..."等；Let it be known that... 译为"特此通告……"。

2. 证明

无论是由国家公证机关出具的公证书还是社会团体、企事业单位开具的证明信，均属于正式文体，因而言简意赅、清晰准确。比如，This is to certify that Wang Bin has been conferred a university teacher certification in accordance with Teachers Law of the People's Republic of China and Regulations on the Qualifications of Teachers. (根据《中华人民共和国教师法》及《教师资格条例》的规定，认定王斌具备大学教师资格。)

证明信或公证书是由国家相关部门、机构或单位开具的，用于证明某种没有争议的法律行为或具有法律意义的时间或文书，如证明当事人的身份、权利、资格、成绩、财力等，因而开具此类文书的前提是实事求是，即证明机关或个人真正了解被证明人的真实情况。因此，证明信函是极其严肃、审慎的文书。

下面通过两个典型任务来练习证明文本的翻译。

任务1. 根据提示将下面的英文证明文本译成中文。

Institutions of Higher Learning
GRADUATION CERTIFICATE

(Bearer's Photo)

　　This is to certify that Zhang Ling, female, Student No. 2011××××, born on October 12, 1992, has specialized in International Business of this University from September 2011 to July 2015, and has completed the four-year undergraduate program with qualified academic standing, and is hereby awarded this Graduation Certificate.

Cert. No. 2015××××　　　　Seal of Tianjin Foreign Studies University
　　　　　　　　　　　　　　　　　　Seal of the President
　　　　　　　　　　　　　　　　　　　　　July 2015

(资料来源：徐雅琴，唐沛. 应用英文大全[M]. 上海：上海科学技术出版社，2009. 有改动)

1. 领会翻译提示

- 注意英、汉证书句式结构的差异；
- 注意汉语证书套语的使用。

2. 写出汉语译文

_____
_____
_____
_____
_____

任务2. 根据提示将下面的中文证明文本译成英文。

在职证明

　　胡飞先生于1975年12月8日出生于天津，现为天津宏远职业学院经济学教授。特此证明。

天津宏远职业学院
2022年3月3日

1. 领会翻译提示

- 注意英、汉证书句式结构的差异；
- 注意英语证书套语的使用。

2. 写出英语译文

_____
_____
_____
_____
_____
_____
_____
_____
_____
_____
_____
_____

接下来，我们结合上面所给的任务，具体探讨证明文本的翻译技能和方法。

由于中国和西方社会文化背景存在差异，汉、英证明文本的格式规范和语言表达习惯往往有很大区别。因此，在翻译证书/证明的过程中，译者要按照目的语读者的认知习惯和语言表达方式进行相应的调整，从而写出与原文功能对等、风格一致的译文。

1. 必要的格式调整

英、汉证书/证明的格式规范有很大的差异，译者在翻译过程中应按目的语的格式要求进行必要的调整。英文证书/证明中的"This is to certify that..."放在证书/证明开头，而汉语的"特此证明"放在证明信结尾。

 例1

Certificate of Educational Background

　　This is to certify that Zhang Xiaolu, female, born in 1991 in Hangzhou City, Zhejiang Province, was admitted into the School of Computer Science and Engineering of Nanjing University of Science and Technology in September 2010, majoring in Computer Application. She graduated from the University in July 2014 with a degree of Bachelor in Computer Engineering.

Nanjing University of Science and Technology
September 3, 2021

学历证明

　　张晓璐，女，1991年出生于浙江省杭州市。2010年9月进入南京理工大学计算机科学与工程学院计算机应用专业学习。张晓璐于2014年从本校毕业，获计算机工程学士学位。

　　特此证明。

南京理工大学
2021年9月3日

2. 语言简明得体

　　由于证书/证明是证明相关人员能力、资格、权利、责任关系的具有法律效力的证件，其用语严谨、规范，措辞准确。在证书/证明的翻译过程中，译者要努力使译文语言简明、得体，格式规范。

 例2

公证书

(2022)沪静证外字第78××号

　　兹证明蒋健成(男，1986年9月16日出生，现住在上海市南京西路1145弄86号1002室)至2022年3月30日止，在中国居住期间未受过刑事处分。

中华人民共和国上海市静安区公证处(盖章)
公证员：黄丽(盖章)
2022年3月31日

> **Notarial Certificate**
>
> (2022) H.J.W.Z. NO.78××
>
> This is to certify that Jiang Jiancheng (male, born on September 16, 1986, now residing at Room 1002, No.86, Lane 1145, Nanjing Road (W), Shanghai) had no criminal record during his residence in China up to March 30, 2022.
>
> Shanghai JingAn District Notary Public Office
The People's Republic of China (Seal)
Notary Public: Huang Li(Seal)
Dated March 31, 2022

3. 恰当使用套语

语言正式、结构严谨的套语常常出现在各种证书、证明中,但英、汉套语的表现方式差异很大。因此,在进行英、汉证书/证明互译时,译者要恰当使用目的语的套语,以便目的语读者理解和接受。比如,汉语证明中常用"特此证明"或"兹证明……",而英文中往往用"This is to certify..."; 汉语毕业证书中的"准予毕业"译为"is hereby awarded this Graduation Certificate"; 汉语职业资格证书中的"授予法律职业资格"译为"is hereby conferred the Legal Profession Qualification"; 等等。

 例3

> **奖学金证书**
>
> 　　王瑞婷同学在2021—2022学年期间,表现突出,德智体全面发展,荣获国家励志奖学金,特此表彰。
>
> 电子科技大学
2022年12月
>
> **Certificate of Scholarship**
>
> In honor of her outstanding performance and all-round development of morality, intelligence, and physique during the 2021– 2022 academic year, we gladly present Wang Ruiting a National Aspiration Scholarship.
>
> University of Electronic Science and Technology of China
Dec. 2022

1. 将下面的中文出生证明译成英文。

出生证明

兹证明王洁(女)，于1999年7月11日出生在中国江苏省南京市，其父王宝明，其母陈思。

中华人民共和国南京市公证处

公证员：张燕

2021年9月5日

2. 将下面的英文法律职业资格证书译成中文。

People's Republic of China Legal Profession Qualification Certificate

This is to certify that Zhang Ming has passed the National Judicial Examination and is hereby conferred the Legal Profession Qualification.

Ministry of Justice, People's Republic of China

Minister: ×××

Certificate Number: ×××

Date: ×××

1. 将下面的中文聘任信译成英文。

聘任信

本校聘请张伟先生担任数学教授，聘期两年，自2022年1月至2024年1月。

湘江大学

2021年12月25日

2. 将下面的英文病假证明译成中文。

Doctor's Reference

March 13, 2023

This is to certify that Mr. Zhou Wen, 45 years old, had an appendectomy on March 6, 2023 in our hospital. We suggest that he should take a two-week rest after he gets out of hospital on March 13, 2023.

Wang Liang

Shanghai Weimin Hospital

拓展翻译技能 / Broaden Translation Skills

熟悉下面的证明文本功能句并将它们用于自己的翻译作品。

(1) Li Jing has completed the four-year undergraduate program with qualified academic standing, and is hereby awarded this Graduation Certificate.

李静修完四年制本科教学计划规定的全部课程,成绩合格,准予毕业。

(2) This is to certify that the bearer has passed Level Ⅱ of the English Translation Examination.

持证人参加英语二级笔译证书考试,成绩合格,特发此证。

(3) Zhao Ming was enrolled in the School of Foreign Languages of Xiamen University in September 2018 and graduated in June 2022.

赵明于2018年9月进入厦门大学外国语学院学习,并于2022年6月毕业。

(4) If you need further information about him, please don't hesitate to get in touch with me.

如需关于他的更多信息,请随时与我联系。

(5) Wang Ling has won the title of Outstanding Student for her outstanding work.

王玲由于表现出色,获得优秀学生称号。

(6) This is to certify that Ma Sheng hasn't received any criminal punishment during his residence in China until May 10, 2022.

兹证明马胜截至2022年5月10日,在中国居住期间未受过刑事处分。

(7) This is to certify that Mr. Qin Shan and Ms. Liu Fang were voluntarily united in marriage on the 1st day of May in the year of Two Thousand and Two and hereby issue this marriage certificate according to the Matrimony Law of the People's Republic of China.

秦山先生和刘芳女士于2002年5月1日自愿结婚,经审查符合中华人民共和国婚姻法关于结婚的规定,特发此证。

(8) Sun Guosheng has successfully completed the Cisco Certified Certifications requirements and is recognized as a Cisco Certified Network Associate (CCNA).

孙国胜成功地达到了思科认证证书的资格要求,被认定为思科认证网络工程师。

(9) This is to certify that Miss Liu MeiYu was employed in our Advertising Department as graphic designer from January 2019 to the end of December 2022.

兹证明刘美玉女士自2019年1月至2022年12月在我公司广告部担任平面设计师。

(10) During the time she faithfully attended to her duties. She left us of her own accord.
在职期间，她勤于职守。她的离职，系出于自愿。

研读党的二十大报告选段(汉英对照)，提升汉英文本翻译技能，培养国际视野、家国情怀和专业能力。

> 教育、科技、人才是全面建设社会主义现代化国家的基础性、战略性支撑。必须坚持科技是第一生产力、人才是第一资源、创新是第一动力，深入实施科教兴国战略、人才强国战略、创新驱动发展战略，开辟发展新领域新赛道，不断塑造发展新动能新优势。
>
> We must regard science and technology as our primary productive force, talent as our primary resource, and innovation as our primary driver of growth. We will fully implement the strategy for invigorating China through science and education, the workforce development strategy, and the innovation-driven development strategy. We will open up new areas and new arenas in development and steadily foster new growth drivers and new strengths.

(资料来源：http://cn.chinadaily.com.cn/a/202210/17/WS6350b1cfa310817f312f29d6.html)
请结合党的二十大报告选段(汉英对照)，撰写本单元学习体会。

Unit Six
商业广告
Commercial

  Learning Goals 学习目标

- 了解商业广告的功能、构成及文体特征；
- 掌握商业广告的英汉翻译技能；
- 熟练翻译商业广告，译文准确、流畅；
- 翻译商业广告时，彰显客观公正和精益求精的理念。

Warm-up Exercises

1. 将下面的英文广告口号语翻译成中文。

(1) Melts in your mouth, not in your hand. (玛氏巧克力)

(2) What can be imagined, can be realized. (香港电讯广告)

(3) Haier and Higher. (海尔)

(4) You will be as charming as the Sunshine. (阳光时尚衬衫)

(5) Things go better with Coca-cola. (可口可乐)

(6) Fresh up with Seven-up. (七喜饮料)

2. 将下面的英文广告翻译成中文。

My hair was dry, coarse, and unmanageable. But from the time I began to use Pantene Pro-V Treatment Shampoo, it has become healthy and shiny. This is because Pantene Pro-V Treatment Shampoo contains unique Pro-V B5, which deeply penetrates your hair from root to tip. Its new improved formula gives your hair extra protection against damage, leaving it healthier and shiner.

商业广告 Unit Six Commercial

文本功能及构成
Structure and Functions

广义的广告泛指各种唤起注意、告知信息、传播观点的公众沟通活动；狭义的广告特指传递产品和服务信息的非人员促销手段等商业推广活动。一般来说，文字性广告由标题、正文、口号和附文组成。广告标题是表现广告主题的短语或句子，意在吸引消费者的注意并激发其购买欲望。广告正文是广告文稿的中心，对商品特点、使用方法及售后服务等提供详细的说明。广告口号指的是名牌产品拥有的简短、醒目的广告语，通常是短小精悍、便于记忆的词组和句子。附文包括商标(trade mark)、品名(name of commodity)、公司或厂家的视觉标记(visual symbols)、公司地址、电话等，旨在强化商品和企业形象，提供联系购买的信息。商业广告通过各个部分的有机结合起到推销商品、激励消费的宣传功能。

广告翻译作为一种跨文化交流活动，不仅要使译文符合目的语的语言特点，还要使其符合目的语国家/地区的社会文化环境，从而取得预期的宣传效果。因此，广告译者不仅要了解商品或服务的源语言文化背景，还要熟悉目的语国家/地区的文化心理、价值观念和审美特点。例如，佳能电子产品广告"Cannon Delighting You Always"译为"感动常在佳能"，该广告的汉译者没有选择英文Delighting的对等中文"喜悦"，而是采用改写策略，用"感动"来代替"喜悦"一词。"喜悦或快乐"与英语国家/地区推崇个人感受的文化价值一致，但它不是中国传统文化的主流价值观。因此，译文采用的"感动"一词符合当代中国人的心理需求。

熟悉文本特征
Learn about Stylistic Features

1. 词汇特征

广告的词汇丰富多彩，但每一个词的选择与使用都服务于"推销产品"这一最终目的，因此它们往往具备鼓动性和感染力。广告的词汇特征归纳起来主要有如下几方面。

1) 创造新词

广告中常用一些杜撰的新词，以突出产品的新、奇、特，满足消费者追求新潮、标榜个性的心理，还可取得某种修辞效果。

例1

What could be **delisher** than fisher? (Fisher渔具)

译文：还有什么比钓鱼更有味？

评析：delisher 来自delicious，与后面的fisher 形成押韵的效果，增添了韵律美。

例2

Give a **Timex** to all, and to all good time.

译文：拥有一块天美时表，拥有一段美好时光。

评析：这是"天美时"表的广告标题。Timex 由Time 和excellent 构成，充分强调了此表的计时准确、品质优越等特点。

2) 使用简单动词

简单动词(特别是单音节动词)经常用在广告中，这是因为它们简练、通俗、朗朗上口，语义既灵活又准确。

例3

We **bring** high technology home. (NEC电气)
我们把高科技带回家。

例4

Everything **is** extraordinary. Everything **tempts**. (Cartier饰品)
件件超凡脱俗，样样新颖诱人。

3) 使用形容词及其比较级、最高级

广告在用词方面倾向于美化所述商品，常常大量使用褒义形容词，以加强描述性和吸引力。

例5

Tender tailoring. **Feminine** but far from frilly... **gentle** on your budget, too. (服饰)
做工，精巧细致；式样，娇美自然；价格，低廉宜人。

例6

> And along the way, you will enjoy **the warmest, most personal** service.
> 一路上您将享受最热情、最周到的服务。

2. 句式特征

1) 使用短语、简单句和省略句

为了达到简洁明了的效果，英文商务广告经常使用短语(名词短语、分词短语和介词短语)、简单句和省略句描述产品和服务，以树立良好的企业形象，表达企业的经营理念。

例7

> Poetry in motion, dancing close to me. (Toyota)
> 动态的诗，向我靠近。(丰田汽车)

例8

> Inspire Greatness (TCL)
> 敢为不凡 (TCL)

例9

> A diamond lasts forever. (De Beers)
> 钻石恒久远，一颗永流传。(戴比尔斯钻石)

例10

> Going East, Staying Westin. (Westin Hotel)
> 到东方，住威斯汀。(威斯汀酒店)

2) 使用祈使句

广告语经常使用祈使句劝说和促使消费者采取行动购买产品和/或服务，以发挥商业广告的作用。

例11

> Let you in a world of wonder: *Pictorial of Science*.
> 让你生活在一个奇异的世界里：《科学画报》。

例12

> Give your hair a touch of spring. (洗发水广告)
> 给你的头发一缕春色。

例13

> Keep Moving (Anta)
> 永不止步(安踏)

3) 使用疑问句

广告经常使用疑问句，目的在于引起消费者的反应和共鸣，从而诱导消费者采取消费行动。

例14

> Need a cleaner that shines without scratching? (清洁剂广告)
> 需要一种光亮而不留痕迹的清洁剂吗？

例15

> Want to be as beautiful as I am? Please use Sifone.
> 想和我一样漂亮吗？请用"诗芬"吧。

3. 修辞特征

商业广告为了达到良好的宣传效果，经常利用各种修辞手法，使广告语朗朗上口、生动形象、耐人寻味，给潜在消费者留下深刻的印象，激发他们购买产品和服务的欲望。广告中经常使用比喻、拟人、双关、对偶、夸张、押韵及仿拟等修辞手法，以增强语言感染力。

例16

Featherwater, light as a feather. (眼镜广告)
法泽瓦特眼镜，轻如鸿毛。

例17

Unlike me, my Rolex never needs a rest. (劳力士手表广告)
和我不一样，我的劳力士从来不需要休息。

例18

A deal with us means a good deal to you. (贸易公司广告)
同我们做生意，肯定是笔好生意。

例19

Natural herb. Pure honey. (蜂蜜广告)
天然药材，纯正蜂蜜。

例20

The only sound you'll hear is praise. (汽车广告)
听到的只有赞扬声。

例21

Hi-Fi, Hi-Fun, Hi-Fashion, only from Sony. (索尼音响广告)
高保真，高情趣，高时尚，只来自索尼。

例22

East or west, Guilin Landscape is best. (桂林风景广告)
桂林山水甲天下。

下面通过两个典型任务来练习商务广告的翻译。

任务1. 根据提示将下面的中文广告译成英文。

> **特仑苏牛奶**
>
> 　　一包好牛奶,是感情与理智巧妙平衡的结晶。这富含天然优质乳蛋白的牛奶,滴滴融入乳牛的幸福。从奶源基地到进入包装,更是对理性的考验,堪称全球楷模的模范工厂。领先世界的先进工艺,确保牛奶闻更香、饮更浓。如此无与伦比的醇香感受,只在特仑苏。
>
> 　　高贵的人生,来自精神和物质的双重给养。用心工作,用心感受生活,以金牌的标准要求自己,亦只感受金牌品质的人生。而此刻,就像我只喝特仑苏。我只纵情这无可比拟的绿色,于天地间放飞自由心灵,这就是特仑苏人生。

1. 领会翻译提示

- 准确翻译品牌名称和行业术语;
- 注意汉、英语句结构差异,确保译文准确流畅;
- 综合运用直译法和意译法,增强译文可读性。

2. 写出英语译文

任务2. 根据提示将下面的英文广告译成中文。

> **Gillette Sensor**
>
> The only razor that senses and adjusts to the individual needs of your face.
>
> Gillette Sensor: the shave personalized to every man.
>
> It starts with twin blades, individually and independently mounted on highly responsive springs. So they continuously sense and automatically adjust to the individual curves and unique needs of your face.
>
> Innovation is everywhere. You can feel it in the textured ridges and the balance of the Sensor razor. You appreciate it in the easy loading system and the convenient shaving organizer.
>
> Even rinsing is innovative. The new blades are 50% narrower than any others — allowing water to flow freely around and through them, for effortless cleaning and rinsing.
>
> All these Sensor technologies combine to give your individual face a personalized shave — the closest, smoothest, safest, most comfortable.
>
> The best shave a man can get — Gillette!

(资料来源：李富森，王耀强. 商务英语翻译(家电方向)[M]. 北京：中国商务出版社，2014.)

1. 领会翻译提示

- 准确翻译品牌名称和行业术语；
- 注意英、汉语句结构差异，确保译文准确流畅；
- 综合运用直译法和意译法，增强译文可读性。

2. 写出中文译文

_____
_____
_____
_____
_____
_____

接下来，我们结合上面所给的任务，具体探讨商业广告的翻译技能和方法。

翻译商业广告时，译者通常使用直译法、套译法、意译法、创译法、增补译法、化简译法等翻译方法。

1. 直译法

译者使用直译法处理的广告口号或标题通常原文意义明确，语句结构简单而完整，按字面意思能同时表达句子的表层含义和深层含义。

例23

> Winning the hearts of the world. (法国航空公司)
> 赢取天下心。

例24

> Life is a journey. Travel it well. (联合航空)
> 人生如旅程，应尽情游历。

2. 套译法

英语中的不少广告借用现成的成语、谚语、短语等来获得文体效果以达到预期目的，译文可以套用汉语中一些现成的表达形式或固定的结构框架，使译文与原文相契合，传达出广告原文的语言内涵。

例25

> One man's disaster is another man's delight! The sale is now on!
> 译文：几家欢乐几家愁！甩卖进行中！
> 评析：这则广告的独特之处在于它采用了仿拟的修辞手法，借用英语谚语One man's meat is another man's poison (甲之佳肴，乙之毒药)，要传达的信息是，不惜血本的甩卖对于商家来说无疑是灾难(disaster)，但对于消费者来说却是令人欣喜的事(delight)。

⬧ 例26

> Tasting is believing.
> 译文：百闻不如一尝。
> 评析：这则食品广告采用了仿拟的手法，巧妙地借用了家喻户晓的英语谚语Seeing is believing(百闻不如一见)来吸引读者的注意，借此展示食品的上乘质量。

3. 意译法

意译法指取原文内容而舍弃其形式，容许译者有一定的创造性，但原文的基本信息应该保存，以传达出原文词句在上下文中的意味。

⬧ 例27

> Good to the last drop. (Maxwell House 咖啡)
> 滴滴香浓，意犹未尽。

⬧ 例28

> We care to provide service above and beyond the call of duty. (UPS快递)
> 殷勤有加，风雨不改。

4. 创译法

很多商务广告都有众所周知的英汉对照的文本，其汉语文本在表层意思上虽然与英语原文相差较大，但长期以来被认为是其英文文本的翻版。因此，我们称这类中文文本为带有一定创造性的译文。

⬧ 例29

> A great way to fly. (新加坡航空公司)
> 飞越万里，超越一切。

例30

> It's all within your reach. (AT&T电讯)
> 联络世界，触及未来。

5. 增补译法

在广告翻译过程中，常对原文某些关键词的词义进行挖掘、引申或扩充，以凸显其深层意思。该方法经常与中文四字成语、习语搭配使用，以提高表现能力。

例31

> Elegance is an attitude. (浪琴表)
> 优雅态度，真我性格。

例32

> Taking the lead in a digital world. (三星公司)
> 领先数码，超越永恒。

6. 化简译法

广告语言应该简练精当、明白晓畅，才有记忆价值。有些英语广告原文具有这些特点，但直译成汉语后就会失去这一特点，译文显得啰唆，达不到应有的效果，因而可以采用化简的方法。

例33

> Wherever you are, whatever you do, the Allianz Group is always on your side.
> 安联集团，永远在你身边。

例34

> Goodbuy winter! 100% cotton knitwear $49.95.
> 换季贱卖！100%纯棉针织服装，仅售$49.95。

商业广告 Unit Six
Commercial

巩固翻译技能
Enhance Translation Skills

1. 将下面的英文广告口号语译成中文。

(1) Challenge the limits. (三星电子)

(2) Intelligence everywhere. (摩托罗拉)

(3) Always with you. (中国电信)

(4) Inspired performance. (英菲尼迪轿车)

(5) We lead; others copy. (理光复印机)

(6) Tide's in; dirt's out. (汰渍洗衣粉)

2. 将下面的中文广告口号语译成英文。

(1) 岁月的皱纹不知不觉游走了。(美加净)

(2) 构建万物互联的智能世界。(华为)

(3) 百衣百顺。(蒸汽熨斗广告)

(4) 心动不如行动。(汽车广告)

(5) 家有三洋，冬暖夏凉。(三洋空调)

(6) 把精彩留给自己。(李宁运动品牌)

91

1. 将下面的英文广告译成中文。

> **The Sheraton Harbor Resort**
>
> Memories bright as a tropical bloom, fresh as a cool sea breeze, and deep as the unhurried sea. Time steps to a different measure here, just for the two of you. The palm bared beach gently kisses the water's edge. Sunset dances; nightlife sings under a star-filled sky; moonlight drips soft silver to tuck you in.
>
> This is the Sheraton Harbor Resort where the days hesitate to end and the memories linger forever.

2. 将下面的中文广告译成英文。

> 欢迎您到四季岛
>
> 　　金色的沙滩，诱人的海鲜，四季岛是男女老幼向往的海滨胜地！
>
> 　　碧海蓝天，风光绮丽，四季岛拥有你所期望的休闲逸趣。在这儿，您可以进行无数种水上运动，也可以悠闲地躺在沙滩上，尽情享受阳光的沐浴。
>
> 　　这儿还有美味佳肴！我们的厨师为您准备了丰盛可口的美食，从广东名菜到华北小吃，应有尽有！
>
> 　　我们还专门为您安排了"环岛一日游"，带给您最大的舒适与享受。您既可以在船上度过难忘的一天，也可以在几处停靠站下船游览，饱览岛上宜人风光。
>
> 　　无论您选择船上的闲憩还是陆上的新奇，您都将度过终生难忘的时刻。
>
> 　　还犹豫什么？

拓展翻译技能
Broaden Translation Skills

熟悉下面的广告套语并将它们用于自己的翻译作品。

(1) 畅销全球　　sell well all over the world

(2) 典雅大方　　elegant and graceful

(3) 顾客第一　　customer first

(4) 规格齐全　　complete in specification

(5) 款式多样　a great variety of models
(6) 美观大方　elegant appearance
(7) 美观耐用　attractive and durable
(8) 品质优良　excellent quality
(9) 效果显著　evident effect
(10) 享有盛誉　enjoy a high reputation
(11) 保暖防风　warm and windproof
(12) 操作简便　easy and simple to handle
(13) 瑰丽多彩　pretty and colorful
(14) 结构坚固　firm in structure
(15) 烹制简便　convenient to cook
(16) 清香爽口　pleasant to the palate
(17) 甜而不腻　agreeable sweetness
(18) 性能可靠　dependable performance
(19) 助消化，除油腻　help digest greasy food
(20) 货源充足　ample supply
(21) 精品荟萃　a galaxy of fine goods
(22) 穿着舒适、轻便　comfortable and easy to wear
(23) 馈赠佳品　ideal gift
(24) 景色宜人　delightful scenery
(25) 闻名遐迩　known far and wide
(26) 口感醇厚　mild and mellow
(27) 交货迅速　prompt delivery
(28) 祛病强身　remove diseases and promote health
(29) 价格公道　reasonable price
(30) 专业设计　professional design
(31) 清仓甩卖　clearance price
(32) 选材精良　superior materials
(33) 技艺精湛　fine craftsmanship
(34) 设计新颖　latest design
(35) 心旷神怡　carefree and joyous
(36) 赏心悦目　pleasant to the eye
(37) 超值享受　unconventional enjoyment

(38) 图案生动　vivid pattern

(39) 柔软防滑　soft and anti-slippery

(40) 历史悠久　have a long history

研读党的二十大报告选段(汉英对照)，提升汉英文本翻译技能，培养国际视野、家国情怀和专业能力。

> 高质量发展是全面建设社会主义现代化国家的首要任务。发展是党执政兴国的第一要务。没有坚实的物质技术基础，就不可能全面建成社会主义现代化强国。
>
> To build a modern socialist country in all respects, we must, first and foremost, pursue high-quality development. Development is our Party's top priority in governing and rejuvenating China, for without solid material and technological foundations, we cannot hope to build a great modern socialist country in all respects.

(资料来源：http://cn.chinadaily.com.cn/a/202210/17/WS6350b1cfa310817f312f29d6.html)

请结合党的二十大报告选段(汉英对照)，撰写本单元学习体会。

Unit Seven
中西菜单
Menu of Chinese/Western Food

 Learning Goals 学习目标

- 了解中西菜单的功能、构成及文体特征；
- 掌握中西菜单的英汉/汉英翻译技能；
- 熟练翻译中西菜单，译文准确流畅；
- 翻译中西菜单时，彰显精益求精和热情待客的理念。

Menu of Chinese/Western Food

热身练习
Warm-up Exercises

1. 找出与下列中文菜名相对应的英文菜名。

(1) 板栗红烧肉	A. Australian Lobster
(2) 百花豆腐	B. Spiced Goose, Chaozhou Style
(3) 澳洲龙虾	C. Smoked Salmon
(4) 扒鲍鱼芦笋	D. Steamed Abalone with Asparagus
(5) 白灵菇鸡片	E. Shredded Tripe with Soy Sauce
(6) 拌肚丝	F. Grilled Lamb Ribs
(7) 北京涮羊肉	G. Beijing Instant-boiled Mutton
(8) 叉烧羊排	H. Mango Pudding
(9) 潮州卤鹅	I. French Apple Tart
(10) 葱爆肉	J. Quick-fried Pork with Scallions
(11) 脆皮香蕉虾	K. Crispy Prawns with Banana
(12) 希腊烤奶酪	L. Greek Grilled Cheese
(13) 芒果布丁	M. Egg Sushi
(14) 罗马风味烤鸡	N. Roman Roast Chicken
(15) 法式苹果挞	O. Bean Curd in Flower Shape
(16) 海鲜椰子汤	P. Seafood Coconut Soup
(17) 日式煎蛋寿司	Q. Braised Pork with Chestnuts
(18) 熏三文鱼	R. Stir-fried Chicken Slices with Mushrooms

2. 将下面的西式午餐菜单译成中文。

Western Lunch Menu

Apple Pie	Biscuits
Chicken Nugget	Cream
Double Cheeseburger	Doughnut
French Fries	Hamburger
Hot Dog	Ice-cream Sundae
Ketchup	Milkshake
Pizza	Pepper
Sandwich	Salt
Lettuce	Sausage
Tomato	Chocolate Cake
Onion	Lemonade

文本功能及构成
Structure and Functions

俗话说，民以食为天。烹饪和饮食艺术是各地历史文化的重要组成部分，也是各地文明的见证和象征。在外事活动中，不管是出访还是接待来访，工作之余或饱览秀丽风光之后，宾客们都要品尝一下所在国家/地区的菜肴。因此，菜单的翻译问题就摆在译者面前。中餐菜单一般由冷盘(Cold Dishes)、热盘(Hot Dishes)、主食和甜品类(Cereals and Desserts)及汤类(Soups)组成。西餐菜单通常由以下六部分组成：冷盘(Cold Starters)、热盘(Hot Starters)、汤(Soups)、肉禽类菜肴(Meat and Poultry)、蔬菜类菜肴(Vegetarian Dishes)及甜品(Desserts)。

熟悉文本特征
Learn about Stylistic Features

1. 中餐菜单

中国的饮食文化源远流长，享有"烹饪之国"的美名。中国菜肴品种繁多，由于各地风俗习惯、饮食爱好不同，形成了多种风味各异的中国菜品。中国菜素有南甜、北咸、东辣、西酸之说。按照地域划分，中国菜由八大菜系组成，即川菜、鲁菜、粤菜、苏菜(淮扬菜系)、浙菜、闽菜、徽菜和湘菜。

中餐菜肴的命名突出美、雅、吉、尚，以其丰富的想象、新奇的寓意、高雅的情趣和深远的意境给人艺术的美感，比如翡翠鲍片(Braised Abalone with Green Vegetable)、梅竹山石(Soup in Chinese Landscape)、如意大虾(Soft-Fried Prawn)、海底捞月(Soup with Jelly Fish and Pigeon Egg)等。翻译菜单的目的是方便对中国文化感到陌生的外国客人点菜，因此需要让外国客人一看到菜单就知道菜的原料和烹调方法。

2. 西餐菜单

西餐是西方式餐饮的统称，广义上讲，也可以说是西方餐饮文化的统称。"西方"习惯上是指欧洲国家和地区，以及由这些国家和地区为主要移民的北美洲、南美洲和大洋洲的广大区域，因此西餐主要指代以上区域的餐饮文化。

西餐菜肴品种繁多，显著特点是主料突出，营养丰富，讲究色彩，味道鲜香。西方许多人认为，菜品的主要功能是满足人的生理需要，即填饱肚子，有一点艺术性，能在一定程度上满足心理需要就足够了。因此，西餐菜品的命名注重写实，兼有少量的写意，内容具体，清楚明了，逻辑性强，比如Cold Roast Beef(冷烤牛肉)、Belgian Stewed Chicken(比利时烩鸡)、Natural Fried Veal Cutlet(清煎小牛排)、Cucumber Salad with Cream(奶油黄瓜沙拉)等。

下面通过两个典型任务来练习中西菜单的翻译。

任务1. 根据提示将下面的中文菜单译成英文。

冷盘

酱牛肉	叉烧肉	熏鱼
松花蛋	酸辣黄瓜	五香花生
小葱拌豆腐	酿皮子	

热盘

狮子头	回锅肉	手抓羊肉
德州扒鸡	左公鸡	糖醋鲤鱼
红煨鱼翅	佛跳墙	黄酒焖大虾
麻婆豆腐		

主食和甜食

锅贴	花卷	三鲜包子
素菜饺子	馄饨	兰州牛肉面
八宝饭	炸春卷	

汤类

龙虎凤大烩	三鲜汤
醪糟汤	西红柿鸡蛋汤

(资料来源：王长春.实用涉外酒店英语表格[M].北京：中国旅游出版社，2013.)

1. 领会翻译提示

● 分析中餐菜名的结构，如原料+作料，烹调法+原料，地名+原料，等等，采用相应的翻译方法；

中西菜单
Menu of Chinese/Western Food
Unit Seven

- 若菜名含有夸张、比喻或人物典故，译者需要了解菜名的文化内涵，灵活处理译文。

2. 写出英语译文

任务2. 根据提示将下面的英文菜单译成中文。

Cold Starters

Red Caviar   Cold Roast Beef
Cucumber Salad with Cream   Assorted Vegetables

Hot Starters

Fish a la Russia   Stewed Kidney with Red Wine

Soups

Creamy Lobster Soup   Tomato Soup with Macaroni

Meat and Poultry

Grilled Prawn   Fried Veal Chop with Mashed Potato
Belgian Stewed Chicken   Soft-Fried Fillet Slices with Onion

Vegetarian Dishes

Stewed Peas with Cream Sauce   Braised Cabbage Rolls in Home Style
Fried Mushrooms with Butter   Curry Vegetables

Cereals and Desserts

Cream Bun   Ham Sandwich
Baked Noodles with Prawn and Tomato   Fried Rice with Tomato and Chicken Cubes
Strawberry Cream-Cake   Raisin Pudding
Mixed Fruit Compote   Ice-Cream Cone

1. 领会翻译提示

- 分析西餐菜名的结构，如作料+原料，烹调法+原料，菜肴颜色+原料，等等，采用相应的翻译方法；
- 西餐菜单上时常有英、法两种文字，比如Fish a la Russia 中的a la为法语，相当于英语的in the，a la Russia= in the Russian style (俄罗斯风味)。

2. 写出汉语译文

接下来，我们结合上面所给的任务，具体探讨餐饮菜单的翻译技能和方法。

1. 中餐菜名翻译

中国餐饮语言受传统文化影响，内容丰富，涉及面广，意趣性强。中国人认为，饮食烹饪应该满足人们的生理和心理的双重需求。因此在命名菜品时，通常以写实为基础，并注重写意。写实命名主要是指直接描述和再现食品的各种外在特征的命名方法，写意命名则主要指具有特殊寓意或象征意义的命名方法。

1) 以主料为主、配料为辅的翻译方法

(1) 主料(名称/形状)+with+配料

例如：白灵菇扣鸭掌 Mushrooms with Duck Webs、番茄炒蛋 Stir-fried Tomatoes with Eggs

(2) 主料+with/in +汤汁(sauce)

例如：冰梅苦瓜 Bitter Melon in Plum Sauce、豉汁牛肉 Fried Beef with Soy Bean Sauce

2) 以制作方法为主、原料为辅的翻译方法

(1) 制作方法(动词过去分词)+主料(名称/形状)

例如：火爆腰花 Sautéed Pig Kidney、北京烤鸭 Beijing Roasted Duck

(2) 制作方法(动词过去分词)+主料(名称/形状)+with +辅料

例如：地瓜烧肉 Stewed Diced Pork with Sweet Potatoes、
青椒牛肉 Fried Beef with Green Pepper

(3) 制作方法(动词过去分词)+主料(名称/形状)+with/in +汤汁

例如：京酱肉丝 Sautéed Shredded Pork in Sweet Bean Sauce、
蜜汁火腿 Steamed Ham with Honey Sauce

3) 以形状/口感为主、原料为辅的翻译方法

(1) 菜品形状/口感+主料

例如：玉兔馒头 Rabbit-shaped Mantou、脆皮鸡 Crispy Chicken

(2) 菜品做法(动词过去分词)+形状/口感+主料+with+辅料

例如：小炒黑山羊 Sautéed Sliced Lamb with Pepper and Parsley、
清蒸火腿鸡片 Steamed Sliced Chicken with Ham

4) 以人名/地名为主、原料为辅的翻译方法

(1) 菜品创始人/发源地+主料

例如：麻婆豆腐 Mapo Tofu (Sautéed Tofu in Hot and Spicy Sauce)、
北京烤鸭 Beijing Roasted Duck

(2) 菜品主料+发源地+Style

例如：德州扒鸡 Braised Chicken, Dezhou Style、
兰州牛肉面 Noodles in Clear Beef Soup, Lanzhou Style

5) 直译与释义结合的翻译方法

翻译一些使用夸张、比喻的菜名和涉及人物典故的菜名时，译者先按中文菜名译出字面意义，然后补充说明其内在的含义。

例如：全家福 Happy Family (A Combination of Shrimps, Pork, Beef, Chicken and Mixed Vegetables with Brown Sauce)、佛跳墙 Buddha Jumping over the Wall (Steamed Abalone with Shark's Fin and Fish Maw in Broth)

2. 西餐菜名译法

西方餐饮语言受其传统文化的影响，体现出内容系统、清楚明了、逻辑性强的特点。西餐菜名多使用两种结构：①名词词组，比如Creamy Lobster Soup(奶油龙虾汤)、Red Caviar(红鱼子酱)、Grilled Prawns(铁扒大虾)等；②名词词组+介词词组，比如Stewed Kidney with Red Wine(红酒汁炖腰花)、Fried Mushrooms with Butter(黄油炒蘑菇)、Braised Cabbage Rolls in Home Style(家常焖洋白菜卷)等。

1) 直译法

翻译由名词词组构成的英语菜名时，译者通常使用直译法。例如：

Curry Vegetables(咖喱蔬菜)、Prawn Souffle(大虾蛋奶酥)、Mixed Meat Jelly(什锦肉冻)等。

2) 换序译法

翻译由"名词词组+介词词组"构成的英语菜名时，根据汉语的表达习惯，译者经常使用换序译法，即译文顺序为"介词词组+名词词组"。例如：

Baked Noodles with Prawn and Tomato(大虾番茄烤面条)；Sliced Salami with Potato, Onions, and Parsley(意式沙拉拼盘)；Soft-fried Fillet Slices with Onion(洋葱软炸里脊)；等等。

1. 将下面的欧陆式早餐菜单译成中文。

Continental Breakfast Menu

Fresh Squeezed:

◎ Orange　　　　◎ Grapefruit

◎ Carrot　　　　◎ Apple

◎ Seasonal Fruits

Selection of Pastry:

◎ Croissant　　　◎ Danish Pastry

◎ Pain au Chocolate　◎ Muffins

with ◎ Preserves　◎ Honey　　　◎ Butter

Coffee:

◎ Fresh Brewed Coffee　◎ Decaffeinated Coffee

with ◎ Cream　　◎ Milk

Selection of Teas:

◎ English　　　　◎Green　　　　◎Jasmine Tea

with　◎Cream　　◎Milk　　　　◎Lemon

中西菜单
Menu of Chinese/Western Food

Unit Seven

_____
_____
_____
_____
_____

2. 将下面的普通西式早餐菜单译成英文。

普通西式早餐菜单

鲜榨果汁：
◎橙汁　　　　　　　◎西柚汁
◎胡萝卜汁　　　　　◎当日时令鲜榨果汁
两只新鲜农场鸡蛋，做法由您任选：
◎水波蛋　　　　　　◎炒蛋
◎双面煎蛋　　　　　◎单面煎蛋
◎煮鸡蛋_____分钟
乡村鲜土豆及烤番茄、香煎草菇、猪肉肠、熏猪肉。精选各色吐司、果酱、蜂蜜及黄油
咖啡：
◎现磨咖啡　　　　　◎无咖啡因咖啡
配◎奶油　　　　　　◎奶
精选茶类：
◎英国红茶　　　　◎绿茶　　　　◎茉莉花茶
配◎奶油　　　　　◎牛奶　　　　◎柠檬

_____
_____
_____
_____
_____

1. 将下面的中式晚餐菜单译成英文。

中式晚餐菜单

杏仁豆腐	中国火腿
海蜇	烧卖
叉烧包	腊肠
芥末	皮蛋
粉丝	蛋挞
辣酱	糯米
蚝油	春卷
云吞	汤圆
虾仁炒蛋	饺子
红豆汤	排骨

中西菜单
Menu of Chinese/Western Food

2. 将下面的西式晚餐菜单译成中文。

Western Dinner Menu

Baked Potato	Coffee Pot
Cake	Crackers
Chocolate Pudding	Mashed Potato
Corn-on-the-cob	Pork Chop
Fish Pie	Roast Chicken
Meatballs	Soup
Roast Beef	Wine
Salad	Steak
Spaghetti	Beer
Cheese	Coffee

拓展翻译技能
Broaden Translation Skills

1. 熟悉下面的沙拉与蔬菜类菜单并将其用于自己的翻译作品。

Restaurant Menu—Salad and Vegetables
餐厅菜谱——沙拉与蔬菜

Ham Salad 火腿沙拉	Cauliflower 菜花
Chicken-breast Salad 鸡脯沙拉	Celery 芹菜

Shredded Chicken Salad 鸡丝沙拉	Cabbage 卷心菜
Egg Salad 鸡蛋沙拉	Broccoli 西蓝花
Fish Salad 鱼片沙拉	Leeks 韭菜
Shrimp Salad 虾仁沙拉	Kale 羽衣甘蓝
Salad Nicoise 尼斯沙拉	Radishes 水萝卜
Gelatin Salad 胶状沙拉	Spinach 菠菜
Sunshine Salad 胡萝卜沙拉	Turnip 芜菁
Waldorf Salad 沃尔多夫沙拉	Peas 豌豆
Vegetable Combination Salad 蔬菜大会沙拉	Chicory 菊苣根
Mixed Salad 什锦沙拉	Asparagus 芦笋
Home-made Vegetable Salad 家常蔬菜沙拉	Fennel 茴香
Fruit Salad 水果沙拉	Brussels Sprouts 球芽甘蓝
Chicken Laesar Salad 卤鸡沙拉	Radicchio 菊苣
Tossed Salad 油拌沙拉	Mustard Greens 芥菜
Cucumber Salad with Cream 奶油黄瓜沙拉	Swiss Chard 瑞士甜菜
Tomato Salad 西红柿沙拉	Rutabaga 大头菜
Beetroot Salad 甜菜沙拉	Sweet Corn 甜玉米
Prawn Salad 大虾沙拉	Summer Squash 西葫芦
Crab Salad 蟹肉沙拉	Pumpkin 南瓜

2. 熟悉下面的饮料酒水菜单并将其用于自己的翻译作品。

Restaurant Menu—Beverage
餐厅菜单——饮料酒水类

Tomato Juice 西红柿汁	Iced Americano 冰美式咖啡
Grape Juice 葡萄汁	Myers's 美雅士
Orange Juice 橙汁	Vodka 伏特加
Grapefruit Juice 葡萄柚汁	Hennessy 轩尼诗
Cranberry Juice 越橘汁	Rum 朗姆酒
Carrot Juice 胡萝卜汁	Brandy 白兰地
Apple Juice 苹果汁	Champagne 香槟
Lemonade 柠檬水	Whisky 威士忌
Coconut 椰子汁	Cocktail 鸡尾酒
Milk 奶	Gin and Tonic 碳酸琴酒

中西菜单
Menu of Chinese/Western Food

Milkshake 奶昔	Martini 马丁尼酒
Honey 蜜糖水	Manhattan 曼哈顿鸡尾酒
Tea 茶	Tequila 龙舌兰酒
Hot Black Tea 热红茶	Vermouth 味美思酒(一种开胃酒)
Hot Lemon Tea 热柠檬茶	Sunkist Soda 新奇士
English Tea 英国红茶	Martell 马爹利
Coffee 咖啡	Red Label 红方
Cappuccino 卡布奇诺	Famous Grouse 威雀
Soda 苏打水	Jack Daniel 杰克丹尼
Sprite 雪碧	Bokma 波克马
Pepsi 百事可乐	J&B 珍宝

聚焦价值引领
Focus on Values Education

研读党的二十大报告选段(汉英对照)，提升汉英文本翻译技能，培养国际视野、家国情怀和专业能力。

> 人民民主是社会主义的生命，是全面建设社会主义现代化国家的应有之义。全过程人民民主是社会主义民主政治的本质属性，是最广泛、最真实、最管用的民主。
>
> People's democracy is the lifeblood of socialism, and it is integral to our efforts to build a modern socialist country in all respects. Whole-process people's democracy is the defining feature of socialist democracy; it is democracy in its broadest, most genuine, and most effective form.

(资料来源：http://cn.chinadaily.com.cn/a/202210/17/WS6350b1cfa310817f312f29d6.html)

请结合党的二十大报告选段(汉英对照)，撰写本单元学习体会。

Unit Eight
旅游文本
Tourism Texts

 Learning Goals 学习目标

- 了解旅游文本的功能、构成及文体特征；
- 掌握旅游文本的英汉翻译技能；
- 熟练翻译旅游文本，译文准确流畅；
- 翻译旅游文本时，彰显卓越服务、文明旅游的理念。

1. 找出与下列中文旅游术语相对应的英文术语。

(1) 豪华巴士	A. airport lounge
(2) 抵达大厅	B. national guide
(3) 套餐游	C. tour group
(4) 候机室	D. duty-free goods
(5) 旅游团	E. deluxe coach
(6) 往返票	F. business trip
(7) 商务旅行	G. package tour
(8) 登机卡	H. round-trip ticket
(9) 免税商品	I. boarding pass
(10) 全程导游	J. arrival lobby
(11) 背包旅行者	K. local guide
(12) 出境游客	L. tour leader
(13) 当地导游	M. travelling expense
(14) 度假区	N. receiving country
(15) 领队	O. outbound tourist
(16) 旅游费用	P. tour route
(17) 旅游接待国	Q. holiday resort
(18) 旅游路线	R. backpacker

2. 将下面的英文旅游文本译成中文。

> Do you wonder what it is like up at the top of Yosemite Falls, before the water spills over the brink? The Fall begins as snow in the granite reaches of Yosemite wilderness. When the snow melts each spring, Yosemite Creek transforms into a free-falling torrent. Watch the comets of spray. Hear the water roar. And from the Lower Fall Bridge, feel the shower of lifetime!

文本功能及构成 Structure and Functions

旅游文本是跨国界、跨文化的一种宣传媒介,主要用来介绍和宣传各地的城市景观、自然景观、民俗风情和饮食文化等。旅游文本种类繁多,形式多样,主要包括旅游宣传手册、旅游标识语、旅游景点介绍、旅游导游词、旅游指南等。由于篇幅所限,我们主要了解旅游景点介绍文本的功能特征,然后探讨该领域的翻译技能。

旅游景点介绍文本通常涵盖旅游景观的历史渊源、风格特色、景观价值等内容。旅游景观主要包括人文古迹、自然风景和自然人文综合景观三类。其中,人文古迹景观介绍文本以历史渊源和文化特色为主要内容;自然风景介绍文本强调优美的景色;自然人文综合景观介绍文本将两者融合在一起,涵盖地理位置、地貌结构、历史沿革、景物特色和综合价值等。旅游景点介绍文本旨在增加游客在人文、历史和自然景观方面的知识,增强其游览的兴趣。它有两个功能:一是信息功能;二是呼唤功能。信息功能是指旅游文本要介绍旅游景点的人文景观和自然景观等方面的信息。呼唤功能是指旅游文本能够使游客产生游览相关景点的强烈愿望。

翻译旅游文本时,译者要明确英汉旅游文本的行文差异,根据目的语的句式结构和行文特点做出必要的调整，确保译文准确通顺、简洁明了，符合目的语读者的认知习惯和审美要求。

1. 英语用语简略，汉语言辞华美

英语景点介绍文本大多风格简约，表达直观通俗，注重信息的准确性和语言的实用性，常用客观的具象罗列来传达景物之美。而汉语文本讲究四言八句，言辞华美，追求客观景物与主观情感的和谐交融之美，大量使用对偶平行结构和四字句，以求行文工整，音韵和谐。

 例1

> 桂林的山，平地拔起，百媚千娇，像高耸云霄的奇花巨葩，盛开在锦绣江南；漓江的水，澄明清澈，晶莹碧绿，恰似翡翠玉带，逶迤在奇峰秀山之间。
> Guilin is surrounded by abrupt rock hills rising straight out of the ground. The hills have a myriad of forms, some graceful, others grotesque. Among them winds the flowing Lijiang River which holds a mirror to them.

 例2

> The youngest of the Rocky Mountains, the Teton Range is a spectacular sight. Enhanced by glaciers, deep canyons, snowfields, and lakes, the range shoots up suddenly, with no foothills around it.
> 虽为落基山山脉中年岁最小的一座，提顿山却气宇非凡。它拔地而起，绝壁凌空，冰川映雪地，高峡出平湖，景色蔚为壮观。

2. 英语句式严谨，汉语语句松散

英语注重"形合"，讲究句式结构的逻辑层次和有机组合，反映出英语表达逻辑严谨、思维缜密的美学特点。而汉语注重"意合"，句子结构比较松散、自由，常常靠意境将篇章内容串联起来。

例3

> Crisscrossed by ferries and carpeted with yachts on weekends, Sydney Harbor is both the city playground and a major port. Its multiple sandstone headlands, dramatic cliffs, rocky islands, and stunning bays and beaches make it one of the most beautiful stretches of water in the world, and offer a close-up of Aussie beach culture and its best.
>
> 悉尼港是悉尼市的游乐场所和主要港口,周末无数的渡船和游艇穿梭于此。它多样的砂岩岬角、引人瞩目的悬崖峭壁、多岩石的岛屿、美丽的海湾和海滩使它成为世界上最美丽的连绵海域之一,淋漓尽致地凸显了澳大利亚的海滨文化。

例4

> 崂山,林木苍翠,繁花似锦,到处生机盎然。其中,更不乏古树名木。景区内,古树名木近300株,50%以上为国家一类保护植物,著名的有银杏、桧柏等。
>
> Laoshan Scenic Area is thickly covered with trees of many species, which add lustre to its scenery. Among them about 300 are considered rare and precious, half of which are plants under state-top-level protection. The most famous species include ginkgo and cypress.

3. 英语客观具体,汉语情感渲染

英语景点介绍文本表达精细、深刻,描绘直观可感,具有一种明快酣畅之美。汉语景点介绍文本用词大多宽泛而深远,行文华丽多彩,主观色彩浓厚,因而景物刻画不求明晰,多带模糊思维的痕迹。

例5

> Look into the distance and you will have a nice view of the White Swan Pond in the Pearl River and boats up and down the river with the bright moon and twinkling stars in the sky.
>
> 夜晚,凭栏远望珠江上的白鹅潭,皓月当空,繁星闪闪,舟楫如梭,鹅潭美景,一览无余。

例6

黄山自古云成海,流动在千峰万壑之中,浩瀚天际,壮丽非凡。峰尖浮海,犹如孤屿,时隐时现,似见非见,瞬息万变,气象万千。变幻莫测的云海与朝霞、落日相映,色彩斑斓,壮美瑰丽。

The clouds float over the mountain and among its peaks and gullies like a sea in which the peaks from time to time appear and disappear, often in the twinkling of a moment, like isolated small island. The cloud sea is even more splendid at sunrise and sunset.

下面通过两个典型任务来练习旅游文本的翻译。

任务1. 根据提示将下面的英文旅游文本译成中文。

CITS American Express, a joint venture company between American Express and China International Travel Service Headquarter, was formed in 2002 and is the first business travel joint venture in China. American Express is the world's largest travel management company with 2,200 travel service locations worldwide in over 140 countries and regions. China International Travel Service (CITS) is China's largest and most influential travel agency with as many as 160 branches or offices all over the country. Resulting from the merger, CITS American Express combines the advantages of the two founding companies and is sure to bring more benefits and excellent service to its customers.

1. 领会翻译提示

- CITS American Express:国旅运通;
- 将介词短语翻译为完整的句子;
- 省译连词。

2. 写出汉语译文

任务2. 根据提示将下面的中文旅游文本译成英文。

> 　　鼓浪屿是位于厦门西南隅的一个小岛，面积仅1.78平方千米，素以"海上花园"的美称享誉中外，是国家级重点风景名胜区。它四面环海，绿色葱茏，环境优美，风光秀丽。它还是全国独一无二的"步行岛"，岛上空气清新，没有车马的喧嚣，却时闻琴声悠扬。岛上居民多喜爱钢琴和小提琴，很多著名的音乐家都出生于此，故该岛又有"琴岛"和"音乐之岛"的雅称。

(资料来源：彭萍. 实用旅游英语翻译[M]. 2版. 北京：对外经济贸易大学出版社，2016.)

1. 领会翻译提示

- 一个汉语句子包含多个动词，将其译成英语时，应恰当处理译文谓语动词和非谓语动词；
- 汉译英时，恰当处理中文句子中的四字短语；
- 根据表达需要，调整译文语序。

2. 写出英语译文

接下来，我们结合上面所给的任务，具体探讨旅游文本的翻译技能和方法。

旅游景点介绍文本属于"信息型文本",其目的在于向游客传递景点的历史风貌、景色特点、景观价值等。在翻译过程中,译者要突出其文本功能,确保译文信息传递的准确性和完整性。因此,旅游文本译文应客观准确、明白易懂,并且具有可读性。

1. 适当增译

在翻译时根据目的语的语义、修辞或句式的需要,适当增加一些词语,将原文的内涵加以引申,使译文更加清晰、流畅,贴近目的语读者的欣赏习惯和阅读心理。

例7

> 三官殿里有一株茶花树,在寒冬腊月开出一树鲜花,璀璨如锦,因此又名"耐冬"。
> There is a camellia tree in the Sanguan Palace blooming fully in midwinter, so it is called Naidong, meaning it can stand bitter cold winters.

例8

> For decades the kingdom of Bhutan has nurtured its image as the world's last Shangri-la. Nestled in the Himalayas, it is a jewel of environmental preservation. Its pristine forests, sparkling, icy peaks, and rare flora and fauna have caused the World Wildlife Fund to dub Bhutan "one of the ecological wonders of the world".
> 几十年来,不丹王国保持着全球最后一个"世外桃源"的形象。这个被喜马拉雅山环抱的王国是环境保护的一颗明珠。它原始森林连片,终年为冰雪覆盖的山峰,在太阳光下,晶莹闪亮,珍奇动植物在这里繁衍、生长。世界野生动物保护基金会把不丹誉为"世界生态保护的一个奇迹"。

2. 适当省译

中文景点介绍文本往往会引用诗词、古典文献,对语句加以强调、渲染,使文章更富于文采,且能引起中国游客的旅游兴趣。然而,对于不熟悉中国传统文化的外国游客来说,这种引用不一定能引起共鸣。因此,在翻译旅游景点介绍文本的过程中,译者要考虑目的语读者的背景知识水平，必要时可以省译古诗词、典故。

例9

湛山寺山门前一对石狮子，雕凿精细。寺外建有"药师琉璃光如来宝塔"，简称"药师塔"。

In front of the gate of Zhanshansi Temple stand a pair of exquisitely carved stone lions. By the side of the temple there stands the Yaoshita Pagoda (the Druggist Pagoda).

例10

正中位置是一座典型的土家吊脚楼，一架梯子搭在屋边，屋角挂着成串的玉米和辣椒。楼的左边是小桥流水，楼的后边是良田美池，一农夫正在扶犁耕田。真是好一幅"小桥流水人家"的美丽画卷！

In the middle is a typical Tujia suspended house, and a ladder is against the wall of the house. Bunches of corns and hot peppers are hung on the corner of the house. On the left, there is a bridge with water running under it, and fertile farmland and a pool are behind the house. A farmer is ploughing the land. What a beautiful landscape painting!

3. 结构调整

英语旅游景点介绍文本通常信息量很大，句式结构复杂而严谨。在翻译过程中，译者往往需要根据汉语"意合"的原则，调整原文的语句结构，化繁为简、化整为零，确保译文准确、流畅，符合目的语读者的阅读习惯。

例11

Here in New Hampshire there are many opportunities to find a peaceful spot hidden among the lush forests of tall evergreens or next to a rambling brook or pictorial lake. 新罕布什尔州森林茂密，绿树常青，小溪蜿蜒曲折，湖边风景如画，到处都是宁静的好去处。

例12

The sky reflected in the water turned the Seine into a lovely shade of blue which trembled in the hazy sunshine filtering through leafy branches of the trees lining the river's edge.
天空映照在水面上，给塞纳河染上了一层怡人的蓝色；朦胧的阳光透过两岸枝繁叶茂的树木，照得河水碧波荡漾。

4. 适当编译

在将汉语旅游景点介绍文本译成英文时，译者在不损害原语信息的情况下，根据英语的行文方式和句式结构进行必要的调整，使英译文内容完整、层次清晰，符合英美读者的认知方式和阅读习惯。

例13

满树金花、芳香四溢的金桂，花白如雪、香气扑鼻的银桂，红里透黄、花朵味浓的紫砂桂，花色似银、季季有花的四季桂，竞相开放，争艳媲美。进入桂林公园，阵阵桂香扑鼻而来。
The Park of Sweet Osmanthus is noted for its profusion of osmanthus trees. Flowers from these trees in different colors are in full bloom which pervade the whole garden with the fragrance of their blossoms.

例14

上海博物馆有馆藏珍贵文物约12万件，包括青铜器、陶瓷器、书法、绘画、雕塑、家具、玉牙器、竹木漆器、甲骨、玺印、钱币、少数民族工艺等21个门类，其中青铜器、陶瓷器和书画为馆藏三大特色。
With bronze ware, ceramics, paintings, works of calligraphy as its distinctive collections, Shanghai Museum boasts about 120 000 pieces of rare and precious cultural relics in 21 categories, including bronze ware, ceramics, calligraphy, paintings, sculpture, furniture, jade and ivory carvings, bamboo and wood carvings, lacquer ware, oracle bones, seals, coins, and handicrafts of ethnic art.

1. 将下面的英文旅游文本译成中文。

> If you long to get away from it all, Donegal is the perfect spot. With soaring sea cliffs that plummet 300 meters, deserted white sandy beaches, jaw-dropping landscapes, excellent seafood, and quiet cosy pubs, Donegal forces you to sit back, slow down, and admire the view.

2. 将下面的中文旅游文本译成英文。

> 乘船游览漓江，从桂林到阳朔，是观赏喀斯特风光的好机会。沿途要经过茂密的竹林、风景如画的乡村、嶙峋的峭壁和山峰。游客也可看到小船上的渔民、鸬鹚和卖热带水果的当地人。

旅游文本 Unit Eight
Tourism Texts

1. 将下面的英文旅游文本译成中文。

> Scotland is a unique and austere place, laden with history, where you can find aristocratic palaces and castles, as well as the traditional parades in national costumes. It has some of the most beautiful cities in Europe, a living testimony of a proud and splendid past.

2. 将下面的中文旅游文本译成英文。

> 长城被誉为"世界八大奇迹"之一，是中国古代文化的象征和中华民族的骄傲。长城的建造始于公元前7世纪的西周时期，并持续了两千多年。它绵延两万多公里，故又称作"万里长城"，是古代世界上最长的防御工事。

熟悉下面的旅游文本功能句并将它们用于自己的翻译作品。

(1) 故宫是中国现存最大、最完整的皇家建筑群。

The Forbidden City is the largest and most complete imperial complex remaining in China.

121

(2) 天坛是由蓝色琉璃瓦铺顶的建筑群，体现了形式与空间的完美结合。

The Temple of Heaven is a blue-tiled complex that displays perfection in form and space.

(3) 西安秦俑博物馆展示了六千多个和真人真物一般大小的兵马俑，他们都按军阵排列而且面朝东方。

The Qin Army Museum in Xi'an displays over 6 000 terracotta life-sized warriors and horses that face east in battle array.

(4) 杜甫草堂是唐代诗人杜甫居住过的地方，他在那里写了二百多首诗。

Du Fu's Thatched Cottage is a place where Du Fu, the great Tang poet lived for some years and composed over 200 poems.

(5) 贵州黄果树瀑布是亚洲最大的瀑布。该瀑布高74米，宽81米。站在观瀑亭，可以一览瀑布全景。

Huangguoshu Waterfall in Guizhou Province is the largest waterfall in Asia. This scenic marvel is 74 meters high and 81 meters wide. You can get a full view of the waterfall as you stand in the Waterfall-Viewing Pavilion.

(6) 亚龙湾是三亚最好的海滩。海水湛蓝，宽阔的沙滩绵延7公里，沙滩后面是棕榈树和青山。亚龙湾海滩是冬夏两季理想的旅游地。

Yalong Bay is known as the best beach in Sanya. It has a wide sandy beach that extends for 7 km along the blue sea, and with green palm trees and hills behind. This beach serves as an ideal tourist place both in summer and in winter.

(7) 木结构是中国古代建筑的基本特点。除了砖瓦以外，中国古代建筑广泛地使用木材作为建筑材料。那时候，木材容易取得，运输方便，经济实用。

A timber framework is a basic feature of ancient Chinese architecture. Ancient Chinese buildings use timber extensively as a building material in addition to bricks and tiles. Timber was easily available, transportable, and practical at that time.

(8) 古代建筑往往用大屋顶和出檐，目的是防止雨水淋湿墙体。自汉代以来，屋檐略微上翘，以保证房间采光充足。

Ancient buildings tend to have a huge roof and extended eaves. This is to prevent rain from dampening the walls. Since the Han Dynasty, the eaves have tended to be slightly upturned to ensure that enough light gets into the building.

(9) 中国茶叶博物馆位于杭州双丰村，此地为龙井茶茶乡。博物馆展示了茶、茶文化、茶历史。此外，游客可以亲自动手采茶，并观看如何泡茶。

The Chinese Tea Museum is in Shuangfeng Village of Hangzhou, Zhejiang Province, where Longjing Tea plants grow. The museum focuses on tea and its culture and history. In addition, tourists may have opportunity to learn how to pick up tea and enjoy watching how tea is brewed.

(10) 传统的苏州园林常常修建在城里，靠近居民区。这些园林把小桥、亭榭的优美，与水、植物和岩石相融合，尽力在很小的空间里再现自然。

Traditional Suzhou gardens are often built in urban areas, near residences. These gardens strive to recreate nature in the smallest of spaces by blending water, plants, and rocks with the beauty of bridges and pavilions.

研读党的二十大报告选段(汉英对照)，提升汉英文本翻译技能，培养国际视野、家国情怀和专业能力。

> 尊重自然、顺应自然、保护自然，是全面建设社会主义现代化国家的内在要求。必须牢固树立和践行绿水青山就是金山银山的理念，站在人与自然和谐共生的高度谋划发展。
>
> Respecting, adapting to, and protecting nature is essential for building China into a modern socialist country in all respects. We must uphold and act on the principle that lucid waters and lush mountains are invaluable assets, and we must remember to maintain harmony between humanity and nature when planning our development.

(资料来源：http://cn.chinadaily.com.cn/a/202210/17/WS6350b1cfa310817f312f29d6.html)

请结合党的二十大报告选段(汉英对照)，撰写本单元学习体会。

Unit Nine
产品说明书
Instructions

 Learning Goals 学习目标

- 了解产品说明书的功能、构成及文体特征；
- 掌握产品说明书的英汉翻译技能；
- 熟练翻译产品说明书，译文准确流畅；
- 翻译产品说明书时，彰显科学精准、质量为先的理念。

产品说明书 Instructions

1. 找出与下列中文产品说明书术语相对应的英文术语。

(1) 规格	A. Getting Started
(2) 性能	B. Operations/Instructions
(3) 成分	C. Expiration
(4) 注意事项	D. Manufacturer
(5) 警告	E. Performance
(6) 安全说明	F. Ingredients
(7) 疑难解答	G. FAQ
(8) 使用入门	H. Warnings
(9) 保修范围	I. Warranty
(10) 安装指南	J. Installation
(11) 储存方法	K. Specifications
(12) 使用期限	L. Safety Instructions
(13) 尺寸	M. Storage
(14) 使用方法	N. Precautions
(15) 制造商	O. Measurement
(16) 经销商	P. Retailer
(17) 最终用户	Q. End User
(18) 零售商	R. Dealer

125

2. 将下面的英文产品说明书译成中文。

> This hairdryer is part of the new Philips Salon Compact range and has been specially designed to offer you comfortable and reliable drying. It has a compact and lightweight design, making it easy to use. Its strong airflow dries your hair quickly, giving it the luster, body, and richness you love. You can visit our website at www.consumer.philips.com for more information about this product or other Philips products.

文本功能及构成 Structure and Functions

产品说明书是厂家向消费者介绍产品名称、用途性能、原理构造、使用方法、维护保养、注意事项等内容的应用型文本。按照不同用途,说明书可以分为家电说明书、药品说明书、化妆品说明书、食品说明书、机械装备说明书、仪器说明书等。产品说明书旨在对商品进行客观、准确的描述,并激起消费者的消费欲望。

1. 产品说明书功能

产品说明书具有信息功能和指示功能。产品说明书的目的在于让消费者了解产品质量、产品性能、产品的使用方法及使用过程中的注意事项等。所以,产品说明书最重要的功能便是其信息功能。当然,在指导读者如何使用产品,告诉读者该做什么,不该做什么时,产品说明书又具有指示功能。另外,一份好的产品说明书也具有号召功能,通过对产品的介绍,让读者了解产品的性能,掌握产品的操作方法,从而激发读者购买此种产品的欲望。

2. 产品说明书结构

产品说明书结构相对固定，通常包括标题、正文、署名三部分。标题部分应列出商品的具体名称，比如"海尔冰箱""汰渍洗衣粉"及"飞利浦剃须刀"等。正文内容涵盖商品用途、性能、特点、用法、维修、注意事项等。署名部分一般由厂商、经销商、电话、传真、网址、地址、邮编等信息构成。通常情况下，产品的性能、用途和使用方法是产品说明书的主要内容。

例1

> Jacob's Hi-Calcium, enriched with calcium from milk, is a healthy and delicious cracker to enjoy at your convenience. It is also fortified with vitamin D. Optimum intake of vitamin D helps your body absorb calcium. An adequate intake of calcium from daily food is essential for strong and healthy bones.
>
> Ingredients: wheat flour, vegetable oil, sugar, glucose syrup, milk powder, butter, milk calcium, salt, flavoring, permitted food conditioner, and vitamins A&D.
>
> 耶谷高钙香脆饼干富含源自牛奶的钙质，是美味可口又便利的健康食品。同时含有丰富的维生素D以促进人体吸收足够的钙。从日常饮食中摄取适量的钙质有助于保持强健的骨骼。
>
> 成分：小麦粉、植物油、糖、葡萄糖、牛奶粉、奶油、乳钙、盐、调味料、食品乳化剂，维生素A和维生素D。

熟悉文本特征
Learn about Stylistic Features

根据纽马克的文本类型论，产品说明书是以传达产品信息为主、以激发消费者购买欲望为辅的应用性文本。翻译产品说明书时，译者必须明确产品说明书的文体特点，才能准确、清晰地翻译产品说明书。

1. 使用专业语汇

产品说明书是对产品进行介绍，指导消费者安全使用产品的文本；翻译时必须做到内容客观真实，语句专业精准，表意清晰准确。否则，读者不知所云，无法顺利、安全地使用该产品，极易造成不良影响和严重后果。因此，译者要确保术语翻译专业规范，信息客观真实。

例2

> As with other penicillin, this capsule may cause occasionally gastrointestinal disturbance, nettle rash, rash, and hypersensitivity reactions.
> 本品副作用与其他青霉素相似,偶尔可见胃肠道功能紊乱、荨麻疹、皮疹及过敏反应。

例3

> 肾功能不全者、血钙浓度过高者忌用,或遵医嘱。
> This product is contraindicated to patients with kidney dysfunction or hypercalcemia. Please consult your physician for questions.

以上两例中,有关产品的医药术语不得出现错误,必须做到专业精准,否则可能给消费者带来严重影响,甚至危及生命健康。

2. 语言简洁明快

产品说明书旨在传播有关产品的信息,使公众在短时间内进一步了解产品的特点和功能。所以,产品说明书在保证提供准确信息的同时,应尽量使用简单句式,使语言清晰、简练。

例4

> 这款洗碗机内配置蓝色LED照明灯,当您打开机门时,所有碗碟便一目了然。不仅具备高效的清洁功能,而且让您完美展示机内器皿。
> 译文:The dishwashers come with internal blue LED light bulbs to make your dishes clearly visible when you open the door. They not only provide the best cleaning performance, but display your clean glassware beautifully.
> 评析:原文中的"让您完美展示机内器皿",通过词性转换法,译为display your clean glassware beautifully,准确反映了产品特性,形容词和副词的使用也使得译文通俗易懂,赋予消费者想象的空间。

例5

Use it once a week and it will nourish your skin deep and remain long effective, making your skin tender and fair.

译文：一周使用一次，深层长效，美白修复，肌肤水嫩白皙。

评析：原文采用的是"祈使句+and+主语+will do sth."句式，结构严谨，符合英文的句法特点。而汉语译文使用四字短语和六字短语，句式简洁明了，增强了可读性和感染力。

3. 行文通俗易懂

产品说明书的阅读对象是广大的消费者，而消费者的文化层次一定存在差异，他们受教育的程度不尽相同，有的甚至识字很少，所以产品说明书应做到通俗易懂、准确全面，以便消费者理解和接受。

例6

先用沸水冲热茶具，然后冲泡茶叶。

译文：Warm up the vessel with boiling water and then pour the boiling water on the tea.

评析：英语译文采用常见词语 warm up、boiling water 和 on the tea，简单质朴，表意准确。

例7

Hazeline Snow is specially formulated for all skin types. It contains moisture—suitable even for the most sensitive skin.

译文：夏士莲雪花膏配方独特，适合各类皮肤。它富含水分，甚至连最敏感的皮肤也能涂用。

评析：英文采用被动语态，结构严谨，语言平实。译者将其译成中文的主动句，使用四字短语"配方独特"和"富含水分"，使得译文简洁清晰，发挥了夏士莲说明书的号召功能。

文本翻译实践
Do the Text Translation

下面通过两个典型任务来练习产品说明书的翻译。

任务1. 根据提示将下面的英文产品说明书译成中文。

> Haier's Pulsator Washer with electronic controls provides the convenience of at-home laundry facilities for spaces where full-size machines are not an option. It is ideal for small apartments, mobile homes, and other places where space is limited. This washer features a durable stainless steel tub and an efficient pulsator wash system with 4 cycles and 4 water levels to accommodate a variety of wash loads. Preset your preferred wash end time and the start time is automatically calculated for whichever wash cycle. Clothes will be ready to go when you arrive home or when you wake up. This unit plugs into any standard household 110 – 120 Volt outlet, and connects quickly and easily to any sink with the included fill and drain hoses and Quick-Connect sink adapter. The lift-and-carry handle adds to portability.

(资料来源：http://www.mydigi.net/soft/search.asp)

1. 领会翻译提示

- 查阅字典以准确翻译相关专业术语；
- 中文译文应富有感染力，起到促进商品销售的作用；
- 适当、合理调整译文语序。

2. 写出汉语译文

任务2. 根据提示将下面的中文产品说明书译成英文。

> **升华牌电热水壶**
>
> **介绍**
> 本厂生产的电热水壶是最新快速煮沸开水及饮料的家用电器产品,适用于家庭及工作单位。其结构合理,工艺先进,并具有热效率高、耗电量少、性能可靠、安全卫生等优点,是您的理想选择。
>
> **注意事项**
> (1) 启用本产品前,必须复核电源线路容量。
> (2) 切勿将插座、插头浸水或溅湿,防止漏电,严禁将壶体浸入水中。
> (3) 严禁少水或无水使用,以免损坏电热管。
> (4) 水沸时注意外溢,防止漏电。
> (5) 本产品只限于电热方式煮水,不得采用其他方式煮水。
> (6) 为确保安全,禁止不接地使用。

(资料来源:房玉靖,马国志. 商务英语写作[M]. 2版. 北京:清华大学出版社,2021.)

1. 领会翻译提示

- 准确翻译电器术语;
- 根据目的语表达需要,调整译文句式结构;
- 翻译"注意事项"时,使用祈使句。

2. 写出英语译文

接下来,我们结合上面所给的任务,具体探讨产品说明书的翻译技能和方法。

产品说明书旨在向读者提供产品信息，同时激发读者的购买欲望。因此，翻译产品说明书时，译者要全面把握其内容结构和文体特点，灵活运用各种翻译方法，尽量使目的语规范、简练、通俗易懂，实现产品说明书的信息传达功能、指示功能和号召功能。

1. 传达原文的技术性和专业性

许多产品说明书的技术性很强，涉及专业面广。因此，动笔之前应首先参考专业书籍，查阅专业词典，或请教有关专家或行家，了解相关的专业知识，弄懂说明书全部内容，以保证不造成翻译错误或说外行话。产品说明书的语言比较简练、直观，译文也应具备这一风格。

例8

> 防紫外线双层玻璃门能够有效阻挡紫外线，使葡萄酒保持最佳的储存状态。
> The best quality vintage wine can be stored safely away from the impact of ultraviolet light, blocked by the UV-proof double glass door.

例9

> Our customers have reported excellent results with this shampoo & body wash in their fight against eczema and other skin sensitivities. A great travel size.
> 该洗发、沐浴二合一产品在防治湿疹与其他过敏性皮肤问题方面效果显著，顾客对此评价极高。该包装为超值旅行装。

在以上两例中，将"紫外线"译为ultraviolet，将eczema译为"湿疹"，译文专业、准确，符合目的语的术语表达习惯。

2. 确保目的语的可读性与感染力

翻译产品说明书时，首先要使译文通俗易懂，准确传达原文信息；其次，应使译文语言简洁、流畅，进而促使产品对读者产生吸引力，更好地提高产品的市场潜力。

◆ 例10

Should you encounter some problems during the installation or use of this computer, refer to this trouble-shooting guide prior to calling the help desk. Look up the problem in the left column and then check the suggestions in the right column.

译文：安装或使用本机时如遇问题，请先阅读本故障排除指南，如不能解决问题，再致电客服部。请在左栏中查找问题，再在右栏查看所建议的解决方法。

评析：原文中的during、to等表示时间和方位的介词在译文中略去不译，使得汉语表达简洁、紧凑，增强了可读性。

◆ 例11

California Baby's light & fresh calming essential oil blend adds to the bathing experience, leaving hair noticeably shiny, soft, and manageable.

译文：清新自然、舒缓安神的加利福尼亚婴儿混合精油为宝宝的沐浴增添了乐趣。使用后，头发明显变得柔和、有光泽、易于打理。

评析：原文具有很明显的广告宣传效果，因而译文应体现相应的语言特点，措辞既要客观又要兼具美感，给消费者带来美好的联想。

3. 使用语序调整法

英、汉两种语言在语汇特征、句式结构、行文习惯等方面差异很大。因此，翻译产品说明书时，译者应根据表达需要重新组织译文句式和段落，使译文流畅、地道、富有感染力，从而实现产品说明书的信息传达功能和号召功能。

◆ 例12

首次使用饮水机时，用户应进行消毒处理，具体方法如下。

译文：Before using the water dispenser for the first time, sterilize the water tank in the following steps.

评析：中文中有三个并列的分句，中文读者习惯于这样的句式结构。将其译成英文时，译者抓住了原文的核心内容，即"用户应进行消毒处理"，将其译成祈使句，同时将第一个分句译成介词短语，将第三个分句译成介词短语。这样，英语结构严谨，表意清晰，可读性强，符合英语说明书的行文习惯。

例13

To store large quantities of new fresh food, a press of the Super button will rapidly lower the temperature of either fridge or freezer compartments.

译文：当储存大量新鲜食物时，按下Super键，冷藏室或冷冻室的温度即可迅速降低。

评析：原文中的不定式短语To store large quantities of new fresh food译成时间状语从句"当存储大量新鲜食物时"；原文中的主语a press of the Super button译为隐含条件句"按下Super键"。译者根据表达需要，调整了译文的词语顺序和句式结构，确保译文表意清晰、言简意赅。

1. 将下面的英文注意事项译成中文。

CAUTIONS:

◆Keep it out of reach of children and keep the bottle upright in a cool place.

◆Do not drink. If it is swallowed, take plenty of milk or water and consult a physician.

◆Avoid contact with eyes. If it gets into the eyes, flush with water for at least 15 minutes and consult a physician.

◆Wear rubber gloves during use.

◆Do not use or mix it together with any other household cleaners or bleaches.

◆Use in well-ventilated areas.

2. 将下面的中文产品说明书译成英文。

> 本机是一款外观小巧、设计精美、携带方便的多媒体小音箱,适用于家居、户外旅游、办公室等场所。不仅能让您随时随地享受音乐带来的轻松,也能为您的电脑、数码音乐播放器、手机等视听产品提供完美的音质。

磨炼翻译技能
Sharpen Translation Skills

1. 将下面的英文化妆品说明书译成中文。

> It moisturizes your skin in hot, cold, and dry climate conditions, taking extra care of your skin against the drying effect of the sun, helping to prevent dry skin and protecting your skin from additional loss of skin moisture.
>
> Wash the face with lukewarm water and evenly rub a little amount all over, twice daily, one in the morning and the other in the evening, and the satisfactory effect will soon be obtained.

2. 将下面的中文产品说明书译成英文。

> **保洁丽(POLY CLEAN)**
>
> 　　保洁丽配方独特，能迅速清除玻璃、窗户及其他硬物表面的污垢和尘迹，方便、快捷。用后不留痕迹，令物件光洁明亮。尤适用于清洁玻璃、窗户、汽车玻璃、不锈钢、瓷器及人造革等的表面。
>
> 　　**使用方法**：拧开瓶嘴，将保洁丽喷于需要清洁的物件上，然后用清洁的纸巾或干布抹拭。
>
> 　　**注意事项**：若不慎此液沾眼，请立即用清水冲洗。如误饮本清洁剂，请即饮用大量清水并请医生诊治。请勿用于漆面。

熟悉下面的产品说明书功能句并将它们用于自己的翻译作品。

(1) Protein and fat are essential nutrients that provide the majority of energy in cat food.

蛋白质和脂肪是猫粮中的必要营养素，也是猫粮中主要的能量来源。

(2) Granisetron is a potent and highly selective 5-hydroxytryptamine (5-HT3) receptor antagonist with antiemetic activity.

格拉司琼是一种强效且具有高度选择性的5-羟色胺(5-HT3)受体拮抗剂，具抗呕吐作用。

(3) Put several drops of this product per liter of water to rinse the fruit or vegetables. Leave the fruit or vegetables in the rinsing water for 5 minutes. Before eating, rinse them with clean water.

清洗蔬菜瓜果时，每升水加入本品数滴，将蔬菜瓜果浸泡5分钟后，用清水冲洗干净再食用。

(4) Due to its unique formulation, Hazeline Snow is suitable for the skin of children and adults.

夏士莲雪花膏配方独特，适合儿童和成年人的皮肤。

(5) To obtain the best performance and ensure years of trouble-free use, please read this instruction manual carefully.

请仔细阅读本说明书，以使本机发挥其最佳性能，经久耐用，不出故障。

(6) Carpets made in Xinjiang are famous for their novel designs and elegant colors. They are loved by everyone who sees them.

新疆生产的地毯图案新颖，色彩雅致，人见人爱。

(7) Perform a skin sensitivity test of 48 hours before using this product, even if you have already previously used a hair colorant of this or any other brand.

即使您之前用过此品牌或其他品牌的染发剂，仍须进行皮肤敏感性测试，48小时之后可使用此产品。

(8) Store away from light in a cool place after dissolving a tablet.

药片溶解后，溶液应置于阴凉避光处保存。

(9) The products can be installed in several types such as cabinet, vertical racks, horizontal racks, and ground placement, and installed with other kinds of power supply cabinet according to the user's requirements.

本产品的安装可根据用户需要采用各种方式，如柜式、立架式、卧式及地面摆放方式，也可以配备其他电源柜。

(10) Special function on this model is touch-screen, TV-out, and multi-games.

这种型号的特殊功能是触摸屏、电视输出和同时进行的多场游戏。

(11) It can play audio and video files in any format, without convert tool. Stable quality and stylish body!

可以播放任何格式的音频和视频文件，不需要转换工具。质量稳定，外形时尚。

(12) It is small in size and convenient to carry; besides, it is easy to operate.

体积小，携带方便，操作简单。

(13) It comes in four/a wide range of colors.

有四种/多种颜色。

(14) It is specially designed for extracting juice from fruit and vegetables.

专门为榨取水果和蔬菜的汁而设计的。

(15) The product will be delivered within three days and has a 24-month guarantee.

本产品保证期为24个月，3天内交货。

(16) We provide free 24-hour delivery and 30-day money-back guarantee.

我们提供24小时免费送货上门服务，以及30天退款保证。

(17) This bike is suitable for children aged 10 – 16.

这种自行车适合10~16岁的孩子。

(18) It has been proved that Lvyuan Taigan is able to produce certain medical effects, namely, to allay internal heat and fever, to reduce hypertension, to regulate and strengthen bodily functions, to relieve halitosis, and to dispel the effects of alcohol.

绿源苔干具有清热、降压、通经脉、壮筋骨、去口臭、解酒等功效。

(19) The product is allowed to leave the factory only after strict examination of its quality.

本产品须经过严格质检，方允许出厂。

(20) The product can be used by men and women of all ages with no side or toxic effects.

本产品适用于男女老幼，无任何副作用或毒性作用。

(21) The essence can supplement moisture in time and help to regenerate cells.

这种精华液能及时为皮肤补充水分，促进细胞再生。

(22) It prevents and slows down excessive production of melanin.

本品能防止和延缓黑色素的过旺分泌。

(23) It soothes out fine wrinkles, diminishes signs of fatigue, and evens out the skin tone of the face.

本品能有效抚平细纹，舒缓皮肤疲劳，平衡肤色。

(24) Smooth emulsion over cleansed face with a circle motion.

洁面后，取适量乳液从面部中间往四周涂抹。

(25) Push the trimmer slide key upwards until it is fixed, and then run the shaver.

将修剪滑面刀片按键推上去，待安装到位后开始剃须。

(26) For its structure and refined process, false use would result in outer net guard damage.

由于剃须刀结构精细复杂，使用时要谨慎细心，否则会损坏外部网罩。

(27) To clean the shaver, press down the blame frame, release button to dissemble the blade frame.

清洁时，按住刀锋框架，按下按钮，将刀锋框架拆下来。

(28) In case of a reaction during the application such as intense stinging, rash, or a burning sensation on the scalp, rinse immediately with lukewarm water.

如在使用本产品过程中，有强烈刺激感、红肿或灼痛现象发生，请立即用温水冲洗干净。

研读党的二十大报告选段(汉英对照)，提升汉英文本翻译技能，培养国际视野、家国情怀和专业能力。

> 江山就是人民，人民就是江山。中国共产党领导人民打江山、守江山，守的是人民的心。治国有常，利民为本。为民造福是立党为公、执政为民的本质要求。
>
> This country is its people; the people are the country. As the Communist Party of China has led the people in fighting to establish and develop the People's Republic, it has really been fighting for their support. Bringing benefit to the people is the fundamental principle of governance. Working for the people's well-being is an essential part of the Party's commitment to serving the public good and exercising governance for the people.

(资料来源：http://cn.chinadaily.com.cn/a/202210/17/WS6350b1cfa310817f312f29d6.html)

请结合党的二十大报告选段(汉英对照)，撰写本单元学习体会。

Unit Ten 企业简介
Corporate Profile

 Learning Goals 学习目标

- 了解企业简介的功能、构成及文体特征;
- 掌握企业简介的英汉翻译技能;
- 熟练翻译企业简介,译文准确流畅;
- 翻译企业简介时,彰显诚实守信的理念并体现企业的社会担当。

Corporate Profile 企业简介 Unit Ten

热身练习 Warm-up Exercises

1. 找出与下列中文企业术语相对应的英文术语。

(1) 母公司	A. unlimited company
(2) 分公司	B. large enterprise
(3) 子公司	C. limited company
(4) 有限责任公司	D. private enterprise
(5) 无限责任公司	E. microenterprise
(6) 国有企业	F. SME (Small & Medium Enterprise)
(7) 控股公司	G. parent company
(8) 跨国公司	H. wholly-owned subsidiary
(9) 独资企业	I. sole proprietorship
(10) 全资子公司	J. branch
(11) 民营企业	K. multinational corporation
(12) 微型企业	L. subsidiary
(13) 中小型企业	M. holding company
(14) 大型企业	N. state-owned enterprise
(15) 公开有限责任公司	O. public limited company
(16) 航空公司	P. power plant
(17) 发电厂	Q. law firm
(18) 律师事务所	R. airlines

2. 将下面的英文企业简介译成中文。

> Motorola has been a global leader in innovation in telecommunications. In China, Motorola has invested US$600 million in R&D, building 17 R&D centers and labs in Beijing, Tianjin, Shanghai, Nanjing, Chengdu, and Hangzhou. The number of R&D staff is about 3 000 now.
>
> Motorola China R&D Institute has now become one of the world-class R&D bases at Motorola. It has also evolved into the largest R&D institute built in China by multi-national corporations.

文本功能及构成 Structure and Functions

企业简介(corporate profile)涵盖企业的历史背景、产品与服务、企业结构、资金状况、销售业绩、研发状况、客户群体和经营理念等。企业简介有助于树立良好的企业形象，推广企业的产品和服务，以及提高企业的竞争力。企业简介的预期译文功能是在目的语语境中使译文读者对该公司及其产品和服务留下深刻印象，最终促使他们采取行动。

企业简介通常包括标题、正文和结束语三部分。其中，标题由企业名称加上简介字样构成，比如"美的企业简介"(A Brief Introduction to Midea)。正文一般包括企业背景、服务内容或产品系列、企业员工和企业结构、企业文化和经营理念、企业顾客群或服务范围，以及企业近期的重大发展。结束语部分通常是合作邀请，表达企业的诚意和希望，有时这部分可以省略。

从语篇类型上看，企业简介属于"信息性文本"，介绍企业概况、主营业务、公司员工、主要客户、公司文化、奋斗目标等。同时，企业简介又具有"呼唤性文本"的特征,目的是对外进行宣传,用最直接而有效的语言让读者了解并做出选择。据此,企业简介具备两种功能:一是提供企业机构发展历程、经营范围和企业文化等信息;二是宣传企业产品和服务,打动消费者。

然而,我们发现国内很多企业简介的英译文本质量不高,其中有不少常见的语法及用词错误,而且,由于译者对汉英企业简介的差异性认识不足,英译文本在英语环境中不能实现其交际效果。因此,译者须明确英、汉两个文种下企业简介的差异,才能成功地进行企业简介翻译。

英文企业简介旨在通过提供信息去说服消费者,促使他们做出积极反应。英文企业简介的内容和行文结构特征有:直入主题,信息具体、实在,用事实和数字说明问题,使用鼓动性语言(如将公司拟人化,使用行业排名等)打动消费者。中文企业简介注重信息功能,主要通过提供尽可能详细的内容,让国外读者深入理解该企业。在语篇特征上,中文企业简介喜用夸张手法,常有笼统、抽象的套话,爱用对仗、排比等修辞手段来获得渲染效果。

由于英、汉企业简介的行文方式存在上述差异,翻译企业简介时,译者应首先入乡随俗,遵循目的语的表达规范和结构特点;其次,译者要采用目的语读者期望的表达方式产出译文,确保译文与预期读者的文化背景、美学期待和道德观念保持一致。

熟悉文本特征
Learn about Stylistic Features

1. 英文企业简介文体特征

1) 词汇特点

(1) 使用简单词语。英文企业简介往往使用较简单的词汇,这样可以使材料浅显易懂,照顾到各个层次的读者及消费者。在翻译的时候,译者应尽量选用一些普通词汇。但由于中文企业简介描述性较强,译者也可采用中文企业简介常用的一些表述方法。

例1

> Metrostav is one of the thriving leaders among Central European construction companies, characterized by sustainable growth of production performance and market value, with management levels meeting EU standards.
> Metrostav 公司是中欧建筑公司中的龙头企业,势头迅猛,其生产业绩和市场价值持续增长,管理水平完全符合欧盟标准。

(2) 使用抽象名词。英文企业简介常常使用抽象名词，让行文看起来比较正式、庄重。与此相反，中文企业简介倾向于具体化，往往以具体的形象表达抽象的内容。因此，英文企业简介中表示抽象概念的名词可以直译；由动词或形容词加后缀构成的抽象名词一般可以转化为汉语的动词或形容词。

例2

Our upstream organization manages the exploration for and extraction of crude oil, natural gas, and natural gas liquid.
我们的上游企业专注于勘探和开采原油、天然气和液化天然气。

例3

Reliability, security, and customer proximity is included in the philosophy of PostBus Switzerland.
瑞士邮政巴士旅游局的理念是安全可靠，亲近顾客。

(3) 使用行业术语。英文企业简介宣传企业的情况与发展，涉及各个行业，不可避免地会出现商业术语和行业术语。在翻译术语的过程中，译者要找到目的语中对应的术语。

例4

The company further manufactures surface-treated textiles, especially waterproof vapor permeability textiles under brand name POROTEX.
该公司还生产表面经过处理的纺织品，尤其是商标为POROTEX的防水透气型纺织品。

2) 句式特点
(1) 使用简单句式。为达到宣传企业的目的，英文企业简介常使用简单句。简单句简洁明了，让读者能够尽快获取该企业的信息。而且，简单句读起来简短、有力，更具有号召力。将其译成汉语时，译者要灵活处理。汉语的断句不像英文那么严格，一般情况下，意思较为连贯的汉语句子中间用逗号而不使用句号。

企业简介 Unit Ten
Corporate Profile

🔷 例5

> GUOMOTEX has a long tradition of manufacturing raw materials for the rubber industry and producing semi-finished product.
> GUOMOTEX历史悠久，为橡胶业生产原材料和半成品。

（2）使用分词短语和介词短语。英文企业简介中的句子多使用分词短语或介词短语作定语或状语，不会频繁使用从句，使文本言简意赅。将其译成汉语时，译者在保持原文含义不变的前提下，可以使用汉语的小分句，从而保证译文的流畅和地道。

🔷 例6

> The company has been in the manufacturing business since 1950, adopting the corporate name of GUOTEX in 1952.
> 本公司自1950年起从事制造业，1952年更名为GUOTEX。

（3）使用主动语态。企业简介属于呼唤型文本，重在宣传和介绍产品和服务，如果使用被动语态，将显得过于正式和客观，无法拉近其与读者的距离。因此，英文企业简介多使用主动语态。在汉语中，被动语态使用得不多，所以翻译的时候使用主动语态即可。

🔷 例7

> Volvo, the Swedish automotive, energy, and food group, increased its profits by 10.9% in the first quarter of this year despite a fall of 5% in group turnover.
> 尽管瑞典汽车、能源和食品集团沃尔沃今年第一季度的总营业额下降了5%，但其利润却提高了10.9%。

2. 中文企业简介文体特征

1）词汇特点

（1）使用描述性很强的词语。英文企业简介注重事实和客观陈述，而中文企业简介注重感情的传达和主观的体悟。因此，中文企业简介多使用富有感染力的词语，尤其是四字成语，有时不惜夸大其词。翻译过程中，译者在保持原文信息和美感的前提下，可以进行适当的简化处理，从而使译文符合英文简介的表述习惯。

例8

本酒店集中国传统神韵和西方现代风格于一体，庄重、富丽、典雅。大堂的8根镀金大柱交相辉映，白色大理石楼梯上方嵌有中国古典雕漆画。
Magnificent and elegant, the Hotel integrates traditional Chinese and modern Western styles. In the lobby stand 8 gilded brilliant columns and over the white marble staircases hang huge classical Chinese paintings.

(2) 使用行业术语。与英文企业简介一样，中文企业简介也会涉及不同领域，经常会出现一些行业用语。在翻译中文企业简介时，译者要找到英文中的相应说法，确保译文准确、通顺。

例9

北京加维通信电子技术公司可独立进行数字多媒体、有线电视、卫星电视、无线通信和宽带等领域产品的技术开发、生产和销售，目前已实现有线电视数字前端、卫星数字电视接收、有线模拟电视前端、微波通信等产品的系列化和完整配套化。
PBI's Beijing Jaeger Communication Electronic Technology Ltd. can independently develop, manufacture, and sell digital multimedia, CATV, satellite TV, wireless communication, and broad band. It has developed series of complete products in front terminal of cable digital TV, receiving of satellite digital TV, front terminal of cable simulating TV, and micro-wave communication.

2) 句式特点

中文企业简介常用含有并列结构的长句，句式比较复杂。翻译的时候，译者可以根据情况，将复杂的结构译成短语，从而简化句式。如果无法将其简化，则需要对其进行断句处理。

例10

酒店由名家设计，风格简约、别致，设施齐全，展现的是一个"干净、温馨"的住宿环境。
Designed by famous architects, the hotel, with simple but unique styles and complete facilities, provides a clean and cozy environment.

企业简介 Unit Ten
Corporate Profile

例11

全聚德创立于1864年,距今已有近160年的历史,是中外闻名的老字号风味饭庄。北京全聚德烤鸭店主要经营挂炉烤鸭和山东风味菜肴,以及独具风味的"全鸭席"。它具有雄厚的烹饪技术力量,拥有一大批著名的烹饪高手。
Started in 1864, Quanjude Roast Duck Restaurant, famous for its specialties both at home and abroad, has a history of about 160 years. The restaurant specializes in roast duck and Shangdong-styled specialties, especially offering the unique "all-duck banquet". With high cooking techniques and a fine tradition, Quanjude boasts quite a number of renowned chefs.

3) 修辞特点

中文企业简介经常采用比喻、拟人、排比等修辞手段,使语言更加生动、形象,给人以美的感受。将其译成英文时,译者应尽可能找到较生动的表达方式,如果找不到,可使用英文中简洁、平实的表达方式,以达到宣传的目的。

例12

一座现代化的钢铁联合企业屹立在东海之滨。
A modern integrated iron and steel complex is standing like a giant on the shore of the East China Sea.

例13

寒冷或阴雨连绵的日子,亲朋好友在瑞珍厚围坐一桌,吃时的热闹、气派,味道的鲜嫩、绝妙,食后的酣畅、淋漓,令人心驰神往、流连忘返。
On cold or rainy days, it is really a memorable experience for relatives and friends to sit at Ruizhenhou Restaurant and savor the atmosphere and the flavor here, and to eat to your heart's content.

文本翻译实践
Do the Text Translation

企业宣传资料作为一种特殊的应用性文本,有其独特的语言结构特征,在翻译的过程中，不但要注意信息的传递，而且要考虑中西文化差异和语言风格差异。因此，译者应该准确理解原文，理清原文框架结构，同时注意调整语序，合理选词，以形成简洁、顺畅的译文。下面通过两个典型任务来练习企业简介的翻译。

任务1. 根据提示将下面的中文企业简介译成英文。

> 华为创立于1987年，是全球领先的信息和通信技术(ICT)基础设施和智能终端提供商。我们拥有约20.7万名员工，业务遍及约170个国家和地区，服务全球三十多亿人口。
>
> 华为致力于把数字世界带给每个人、每个家庭、每个组织，构建万物互联的智能世界。让无处不在的连接，成为人人平等的权利，成为智能世界的前提和基础；为世界提供最强算力，让云无处不在，让智能无所不及；构建强大的数字平台，帮助所有行业和组织变得更加灵活、高效、生机勃勃；通过人工智能重新定义用户体验，让消费者在家居、出行、办公、影音娱乐、运动健康等全场景获得极致的个性化智慧体验。
>
> 华为本身专注于ICT基础设施和智能终端领域。通过开放式合作与创新，我们帮助促进和保护全球标准统一，建设产业生态系统联盟，支持全球化开源项目，推进关键技术的突破。我们携手全球各地的行业伙伴，共同构建开放的全球生态系统，推动ICT产业的可持续发展。

(资料来源：http://www.huawei.com/cn)

1. 领会翻译提示

- 将中文语句译成英文时，注意谓语动词的选择和结构安排；
- 根据表达需要，采用合句法，使英译文简洁、紧凑；
- 注意限制性定语从句的运用。

2. 写出英语译文

企业简介 Corporate Profile — Unit Ten

任务2. 根据提示将下面的英文企业简介译成中文。

> COMAC(中国商飞公司) functions as the main vehicle in implementing large passenger aircraft programs in China. It is also mandated with the overall planning of developing trunk liner and regional jet programs and realizing the industrialization of trunk liners in China. It is mainly engaged in the research, manufacturing, and flight test of trunk liners and related products, as well as marketing, servicing, leasing, and operations of trunk liners.
>
> Formed and operated according to the standards of modern enterprise system, COMAC adopts an "airframer-supplier" model, focusing on aircraft design, R&D, final assembly, manufacturing, marketing, customer service, airworthiness certification, and supplier management. It adheres to the principle of "Development with Chinese Characteristics" and attaches great importance to technological progress self-reliant advancement in the process of marketing, integration, industrialization, and internationalization. It manufactures large passenger aircraft that are safer, cost-effective, comfortable, and environment-friendly. It is determined to independently build large Chinese passenger aircraft.

(资料来源：http://english.comac.cc/aboutus/introduction/)

1. 领会翻译提示

- 将英文长句译成中文时，时常运用分句法；
- 英文中，过去分词短语时常表示伴随情况，可根据表达需要将其译成汉语分句；
- 注意中、英文之间的差异——英文客观平实，中文注重渲染。

2. 写出汉语译文

接下来，我们结合上面所给的任务，具体探讨企业简介的翻译技能和方法。

1. 运用类比译法

中国和西方国家/地区在语言文化和认知结构上存在差异，中文企业简介中出现的文化负载词语具有浓厚的中国文化色彩，如果直译成英语，会使西方读者感到不知所云。为了使英语文本在西方文化中达到预期目的，译者应尽可能采用英语语境中类似的表达方式，使译文符合目的语读者的认知习惯和美学期待。

例13

> 珠海华骏大酒店是一座具有欧陆风格的豪华大酒店，坐落在美丽的拱北市夏湾，与海关联检大楼仅一箭之遥，是闹市中的"世外桃源"。
>
> **译文**：Hua Jun Hotel is a European-style luxury hotel and it is situated in Gongbei Summer Bay in the beautiful Zhuhai City. Within a stone's throw from the Joint Inspection Station, it is a land of Shangri-La of the city.
>
> **评析**：大多数中国读者知道"世外桃源"出自晋代文学家陶渊明的名篇《桃花源记》，喻指"环境清幽、生活安闲的人间天堂"。但是该词语在英语中没有完全对等的表达，因此译者采用英语中类似的词语 land of Shangri-La 来传情达意。

2. 信息真实、准确

译者在翻译企业简介时，无论是采用直译法还是意译法，都要努力使译文真实、准确地再现原文内容，并且语言流畅，符合目的语表达习惯。

例14

> 公司是经国家外贸部门批准成立的从事进出口贸易的专业贸易公司。
>
> **译文**：It is a professional import and export company approved by competent authorities of foreign trade and economic cooperation.
>
> **评析**：此句译者采用直译法，英文语序基本上和中文一致，清晰、准确地再现了原文要表达的信息。

例15

> As an outstanding corporate citizen, Walmart actively gives back to the community and has donated funds and in-kind support worth more than RMB 26 million to local charities and welfare organizations over the past ten years.
>
> **译文**：作为一个出色的企业公民，沃尔玛自进入中国起就积极开展社区服务和慈善公益活动，十年累计向各种慈善公益机构捐献了两千六百多万元的物品和资金。
>
> **评析**：如果将gives back to the community译为"回报社会"，没有问题，但若结合下文中的捐赠活动，将译文具体化为"开展社区服务和慈善公益活动"，能使其显得更加贴切。

3. 译文通顺、规范

企业宣传材料在很大程度上相当于广告文本，要求译文必须通俗易懂，符合规范，杜绝文理不通、结构混乱、逻辑不清的现象。

例16

> 公司的进口业务涉及高档化妆品、化妆品原料和美容仪器等，主要从美国进口，年进口额上千万美元。
>
> **译文**：Its imports cover top-quality cosmetics, raw materials for cosmetics, and beautification equipment, the major of which are imported from the United States, with the annual import volume amounting to more than US$10 million.
>
> **评析**：将"主要从美国进口"译成英文时，译者用the major of which引出非限制性定语从句，体现了英语句式结构严谨的特点。

例17

Today, there are 86 units in 46 cities, with a total investment of over RMB 1.7 billion. Across China Walmart employs over 38 000 associates.

译文：沃尔玛目前已经在中国46个城市开设了86家商场。沃尔玛至今在华的总投资额达17亿元人民币，创造了三万八千多个就业机会。

评析：若将employs over 38 000 associates译为"雇用了三万八千多名员工"，语气略显生硬，为使译文更加亲切并增强其感染力，可将其译成"创造了三万八千多个就业机会"。

例18

福建福日电子有限公司是由福建福日集团独家创立的国有控股上市公司，于1999年5月正式挂牌上市。

译文：Floated on the stock exchange in May 1999, Fujian FURI Electronics is a state-owned holding company founded by Fujian FURI Group.

评析：本例将"正式挂牌上市"译为过去分词短语floated on the stock exchange，结构紧凑合理、清晰简练。

4. 调整译文结构

由于中国和西方国家/地区在文化背景、企业经营特色、产品特点等方面各不相同，译者在翻译过程中要深入了解该公司的情况，抓住特色要点，准确表述，必要时调整译文结构，做到主次分明，增强表达效果。

例19

美体考究(宁波)化妆品有限公司成立于2003年，是美国考究股份有限公司在中国设立的子公司。公司注册资金306万美元，具有独立的法人资格。

译文：BodyWave (Ningbo) Cosmetics Co., Ltd. is a subsidiary established in China in 2003 by American BodyWave Shareholding Co., Ltd., with the registered capital of US$ 3.06 million and the independent status of a legal person.

评析：译者将中文第二句译成了with介词短语，译文简洁紧凑、可读性强。

例20

Forty-four years later, Walmart serves more than 176 million customers per week. It is the world's largest private employer and retailer with over 1.9 million associates worldwide and about 6 800 stores in 14 countries/regions.

译文：经过44年的发展，沃尔玛公司已经成为世界上最大的私人企业和连锁零售商。目前，沃尔玛在全球开设了近6 800家商场，员工总数超190万人，分布在全球14个国家/地区。每周光临沃尔玛的顾客超过1.76亿人次。

评析：译者突出了信息焦点"世界上最大的私人企业和连锁零售商"，然后描述商场数量、员工数量、分布国家/地区及顾客人次等具体信息。这样，译文信息主次分明，层次清楚，表达效果良好。

5. 调节渲染程度

英译汉时，译者在保留原文信息的同时，可适当提升其美感和渲染程度，以增强译文的可读性和感染力；汉译英时，译者在保留原文信息的同时，可适当降低其美感和渲染程度，以确保译文客观平实、简洁流畅。

例21

In China, as elsewhere, we follow the Walmart tradition of building our business one store and one customer at a time. We strive to provide our customers with friendly service and a wide selection of quality products at Every Day Low Prices.

译文：与在世界其他地方一样，沃尔玛在中国始终坚持公司的优良传统，即专注于开好每一家店，服务好每一位顾客，奉行"天天平价"的宗旨。始终为顾客提供优质廉价、品种齐全的商品和友善的服务。

评析：本例将follow the Walmart tradition of译成"始终坚持公司的优良传统"，将at Every Day Low Prices译为"奉行'天天平价'的宗旨"，可见英文企业简介客观平实，中文企业简介着力渲染。

公司本着"关怀、事业、分享"的企业文化和"信誉第一、顾客至上"的企业宗旨,竭诚与国内外广大客商携手共进,共创美好未来。

译文:With its corporate culture of "Care, Cause, and Share" and its service philosophy of "Reputation and Customer Priority", this Company would like to cooperate with its partners at home and abroad to create a more prosperous future.

评析:在这句中,将"竭诚与国内外广大客商携手共进"译为 would like to cooperate with its partners at home and abroad,将"共创美好未来"译为 to create a more prosperous future,清晰、简练地表达了原文信息。

1. 将下面的中文企业简介译成英文。

　　天津奥克优(Okeyou)国际贸易有限公司是一家从事精细化工产品及有机化工原料进出口贸易的专业公司。本公司享有进出口经营权和天津港保税区内的各项优惠政策,拥有雄厚的经济实力。

　　天津奥克优国际贸易有限公司经营范围广泛,包括石油化工产品、机电设备及配件、电子产品、五金产品、塑料制品和纸制品等。

　　我们有足够的信心以优质的产品和合理的价格为客户带来更丰厚的利润。天津奥克优国际贸易有限公司愿与海内外各界朋友共创美好未来。

2. 将下面的英文企业简介译成中文。

Kraft Foods Inc. is a global leader in food and beverage. Built on more than 100 years of quality and innovation, Kraft has grown to become the largest food and beverage company in North America were second largest in the world, marketing many popular brands in 150 countries and regions. In 2008 we were ranked as No. 195 in Fortune 500 company list.

In China, we have a lot of well-branded products to suit different needs of consumers, such as Pacific, Oreo, Chip Ahoy, Ritz, Tang, Maxwell, Miracle Whip, etc. Our China Head Office is in Shanghai, and besides Shanghai, we also have manufacturing sites in Guangzhou, Jiangmen, Suzhou, Beijing, and Tianjin to provide our excellent service by preparing good and tasty snacks, beverage, and food for our customers.

1. 将下面的中文企业简介译成英文。

> 白天鹅宾馆坐落在广州闹市中的"世外桃源"——榕荫如盖、历史悠久的沙面岛的南边，濒临三江汇聚的白鹅潭。宾馆主体有34层，独特的庭院式设计与周围优雅的环境融为一体，实为商旅人士下榻的最佳之处。
>
> 白天鹅宾馆拥有843间精心设计的客房，无论是标准房、豪华套房还是商务房，室内装潢设计都经过精心打造，处处显示出以客为先的服务风范。从客房您可饱览广州市容和珠江美景。
>
> 别具特色的中/西食府为您提供中/西式精美菜肴。多功能国际会议中心是举办各类大/小型会议、中/西式酒会、餐舞会的理想场所。另有健康中心、美容发型中心、商务中心、票务中心等配套设施。
>
> 一直以来，白天鹅宾馆将经营管理的发展和高科技成果相结合，使宾馆的服务水平紧跟国际酒店发展的潮流。无论您是到此公干，还是度假旅游，白天鹅宾馆都是您的最佳选择。

2. 将下面的英文企业简介译成中文。

On any day, 2.5 billion people use Unilever products to look good, feel good, and get more out of life — giving us a unique opportunity to build a brighter future.

Great products from our range of more than 400 brands give us a unique place in the lives of people all over the world.

When consumers reach for nutritionally balanced food or indulgent ice creams, affordable soaps that combat disease, luxurious shampoos, or everyday household care products, there is a good chance that the brand they pick is one of ours. Seven out of every ten households around the world contain at least one Unilever product, and our range of world-leading, household-name brands includes Lipton, Knorr, Dove, Axe, Hellmann's, and Omo. Trusted local brands designed to meet the specific needs of consumers in their home market include Pureit and Suave.

Whatever the brand is, wherever it is bought, we're working to ensure that it plays a part in helping fulfill our purpose as a business — making sustainable living commonplace.

We want our business to grow but we recognize that growth at the expense of people or the environment is both unacceptable and commercially unsustainable. Sustainable growth is the only acceptable model for our business.

1. 熟悉下面的短语并将它们用于自己的翻译作品。

(1) be founded/established in...(place/time)　成立于……(地点/时间)

(2) a global Fortune 100 company　世界财富百强公司之一

(3) be committed to providing...　致力于提供……

(4) make consistent efforts and contributions　不懈地努力、贡献

(5) expand business　扩大业务范围

(6) since the earliest days of establishment　自创建初期

(7) aim principally at...　以……为首要目标

(8) adopt a consistent policy of...　一贯秉持……原则

(9) be in line with international standards　符合国际标准

(10) be abundant in... resources　……资源丰富

(11) utilize the natural advantage of...　利用……天然优势

(12) maintain close contacts with...　与……保持密切联系

(13) offer the best services to...　为……提供精心服务

(14) be awarded the gold prize　获得金奖

(15) pass/gain/be granted the Certificate of ISO9002 Quality Management System　通过ISO9002质量管理体系认证

(16) have a general asset of ..., annual turnover of... and an annual trading value of ...　现有资产总额……，年营业额……，年贸易额……

(17) manufacture a wide range of...　生产一系列的……

(18) be ranked second in the world　世界排名第二

(19) be located in/situated in...　地处/坐落于……

(20) engage in/handle a large range of business including...　主营业务广泛，包括……

(21) specialize in...　专门从事……

(22) cover an area of...　占地面积……

(23) adhere to the operation philosophy...　秉承……的经营理念

(24) be headquartered in...　总部设在……

2. 熟悉下面的企业简介功能句并将它们用于自己的翻译作品。

(1) For three consecutive years since 1990, our company has been listed as one of the top 30 enterprises among China's 500 largest foreign trade companies in import-export volumes.

自1990年起，公司已连续三年在中国进出口额最大的500家外贸企业中进入前30名。

(2) This Company has a long history, rich experience, and reliable reputation.

本公司历史悠久，经验丰富，信誉可靠。

(3) We start with impeccable quality to provide exceptional value. Then we add a special personal touch.

我们为您提供超值的服务，是从确保产品完美的品质开始的，其次是我们特有的人性化服务。

(4) Our products rank first among similar products.

我们的产品居同类产品之魁首。

(5) Its unique design makes its "Xinxing" Brand jacket sell as far as to more than 30 countries and regions in the world, all well received by the broad users at home and abroad.

其独特的设计使其"新星"牌夹克产品远销世界三十多个国家和地区，深受国内外广大用户的欢迎。

(6) Time Warner Inc., created in 1990, is one of the largest media and entertainment corporation in the world.

时代华纳公司成立于1990年，是世界上最大的传媒和娱乐公司之一。

(7) The factory can produce various new types of buttons in thousands of different designs for coats, suits, fashions, shirts, and sweaters.

该厂能生产用于大衣、西装、时装、衬衣、毛衣等不同类型服装的上千花色品种的纽扣，产品规格齐全、品种繁多、造型新颖。

(8) Through the leading manufacture, research and development, Samsung has become one of the world's fastest-growing groups.

由于研发、制造方面的领先优势，三星集团已成为世界上增长速度最快的集团之一。

(9) After just a few years of pioneering efforts, the company has achieved an annual output value of over four hundred million dollars in 2013.

经过几年的开创性努力，本公司2013年的产值已超过4亿美元。

(10) Friends and business partners all over the world are welcome to establish business ties with us on the basis of equality and mutual benefit so that they can enjoy sincere cooperation and joint development with us.

我们热忱欢迎世界各地的工商界朋友，在平等互利的原则下与我们建立业务联系，真诚合作，共同发展。

(11) The company boasts tremendous technological strength with well-qualified management and staff.

本公司拥有雄厚的技术力量和专业的管理人才。

(12) We have been in the silk garment trade for 35 years. Our products find a ready market in over 50 countries and regions.

我们厂生产的丝绸服装已有35年的悠久历史，产品大量销往五十多个国家和地区。

(13) Not only are we at the forefront of electronics, but we've received world-wide recognition for our advances in chemicals and engineering as well.

我们不仅处于电子技术的前沿，而且因在化工和工程技术方面取得的进展而得到了世界范围的认可。

(14) In 2012, this Group was listed as the 114th of the world top 500 enterprises.

2012年，本集团在世界企业500强中名列第114位。

(15) We are known around the world as the company that helps our customers save more money so they can live better.

我们公司以"为顾客省钱，从而使他们生活得更好"而著称于世。

研读党的二十大报告选段(汉英对照)，提升汉英文本翻译技能，培养国际视野、家国情怀和专业能力。

全党必须牢记，坚持党的全面领导是坚持和发展中国特色社会主义的必由之路，中国特色社会主义是实现中华民族伟大复兴的必由之路，团结奋斗是中国人民创造历史伟业的必由之路，贯彻新发展理念是新时代我国发展壮大的必由之路，全面从严治党是党永葆生机活力、走好新的赶考之路的必由之路。

All of us in the Party must remember: Upholding the Party's overall

> leadership is the path we must take to uphold and develop socialism with Chinese characteristics; building socialism with Chinese characteristics is the path we must take to realize the rejuvenation of the Chinese nation; striving in unity is the path the Chinese people must take to create great historic achievements; implementing the new development philosophy is the path China must take to grow stronger in the new era; and exercising full and rigorous self-governance is the path the Party must take to maintain its vigor and pass new tests on the road ahead.

(资料来源:http://cn.chinadaily.com.cn/a/202210/17/WS6350b1cfa310817f312f29d6.html)

请结合党的二十大报告选段(汉英对照),撰写本单元学习体会。

Unit Eleven
会展文本
MICE Texts

 Learning Goals 学习目标

- 了解会展文本的功能、构成及文体特征;
- 掌握会展文本的英汉翻译技能;
- 熟练翻译会展文本,译文准确流畅;
- 翻译会展文本时,彰显精心策划、互利共赢的理念。

1. 找出与下列中文会展术语相对应的英文术语。

(1) 保险会议	A. incentive meeting
(2) 分销商会议	B. sales-oriented exhibition
(3) 管理层会议	C. international show
(4) 欢迎招待会	D. cross-industrial show
(5) 技术会议	E. garden and patio show
(6) 奖励会议	F. individual presentation
(7) 销售型展览	G. group presentation
(8) 国际性展览	H. trade association
(9) 跨行业展	I. exposition service contractor
(10) 露天展览	J. exhibit producer
(11) 个人展	K. meeting planner
(12) 团体展	L. service contractor
(13) 行业协会	M. official hotel
(14) 展会承包商	N. technical meeting
(15) 展位搭建商	O. welcome reception
(16) 会议策划人	P. management meeting
(17) 服务承包商	Q. dealer meeting
(18) 指定接待酒店	R. insurance meeting

2. 翻译下列会展名称。

(1) 第五届中国国际进口博览会

(2) International Restaurant & Food Service Show of New York

(3) Canadian Mining and Industrial Expo, Sudbury, Ontario

(4) The 10th International Auto show, Guangzhou, China

(5) 2019亚洲大学校长论坛

(6) CHINA INTERNATIONAL TRAVEL MART 2019

(7) 第八届全球旅游峰会

(8) China's Ninth International Symposium on Intercultural Communication

文本功能及构成
Structure and Functions

  会展是会议、展览、大型活动等集体性的商业或非商业活动的简称。会展(meetings, incentives, conventions, and exhibitions/events，简称MICE)包括会议、奖励旅游、展览会和节事活动四大部分。随着改革开放的不断深入，中国会展业迅猛发展，带动了旅游、运输、酒店、商贸、广告、印刷、保险等行业，取得了令人瞩目的经济效益和社会效益。在会展业的发展过程中，会展翻译发挥了重要作用。一方面，会展翻译为会展活动提供必要的服务；另一方面，精准的会展翻译能够有效地提升中国会展活动的影响力。

  国际会展活动大致由会展策划、会展运作和会展测评三个阶段构成。每个阶段涉及不同的文本，其句式结构和语言功能不尽相同。具体而言，会展文本主要包括会展推广文本、会展服务文本、会展合同和会展报告。

1. 会展推广文本

会展推广是指主办方将会议和展览的背景情况、特色和规模等情况告知客户,并邀请他们参加会议和展览。会展推广文本有相对固定的一套程式化的句式和语汇。在翻译过程中,译者要注意其功能性,清晰、简练地表达原文内容,同时使其符合目的语的表达习惯,从而取得理想的宣传效果。

例1

> The World Economic Forum is an independent, international organization incorporated as a Swiss not-for-profit foundation. We are striving towards a world-class corporate governance system where values are as important a basis as rules. Our motto is Entrepreneurship in the global public interest. We believe that economic progress without social development is not sustainable, while social development without economic progress is not feasible.
>
> 世界经济论坛是个独立的国际组织,以瑞士一家非营利基金会的形式成立。我们致力于建立一个世界领先水平的企业治理机制,使价值成为与规则同等重要的基石。我们的准则是"以全球公众利益为本的企业家精神"。我们认为,没有社会发展的经济进步是不可持续的,而没有经济进步的社会发展又是不可行的。

2. 会展服务文本

在参会者、参展商和买家完成了报名程序后,会展的主办方还应提供一系列有关展会服务的信息,包括到达展会地点的交通信息、展位信息、现场服务信息、展会之后的旅游信息等,协助参展人员、客户顺利参展并取得预期的经济效益。会展服务文本属于信息型文本,因此译者要确保译文表意清晰、结构合理,并且要在语言中体现出一定的服务热情和真诚,从而达到预期的翻译效果。

例2

> You will have been given a name badge upon registration. For security reasons, and as a courtesy to other delegates, please ensure that you wear these at all time. If you misplace your badge, please ask for another one at the registration desk. If you are not wearing a badge, you may be asked for identification.
>
> 您将会在注册处收到胸牌。出于安全考虑,以及对其他与会代表的尊重,请务必始终佩戴该胸牌。如果遗失胸牌,请在注册处申请领取新的胸牌。若没有佩戴胸牌,可能会被要求查验身份。

3. 会展合同

会展合同是指平等的主体之间围绕会展活动，依法订立的各类民事合同的总称，包括会展组织机构与其他会展参与者之间依法签订的设立、变更、终止各方民事权利、义务关系的书面协议。会展合同的突出语言特色是高度程式化的格式，有鲜明的结构层次，以更加准确地表达法律规定的具体内容并保持内容的合理性和规范性，符合专业人员的阅读习惯和阅读期待。因此，译者应遵循合同文本的语言特色和文体风格，使译文专业、精准。对于会展合同中的专用术语，比如出租方(lessor)、承租方(lessee)、争议解决(settlement of disputes)、不可抗力(force majeure)等，译者在翻译中要做到精准对应。在句子层面，译文句式必须符合相关条文的逻辑结构，以便实现会展合同的功能。

例3

> As the Customs requires the official forwarder to be responsible for every exhibit, exhibitors should not be allowed to take any of their exhibits out of the exhibition site before, during, and after the exhibition without prior arrangement with the Customs through us. We shall not be responsible for any confiscation and fines arising therefrom.
>
> 由于海关要求运输总代理对每件展品负责，因此如果没有通过我司向海关做事先安排，参展商不得在展会开幕前、展会期间及结束后将任何展品带出展览中心。对于由此造成的任何展品没收和罚款，我司概不负责。

4. 会展报告

会展报告是主办方在会展之后所做的总结。首先，会展报告涉及会展名称、时间、地点、组织者和参展人员等；其次，总结会议、展览活动的开展情况，看其是否达到了会展的预期目标；再次，会展报告要对下一次会展进行宣传和展望，从而吸引更多的参会、参展人员和买家。会展报告通常用语比较正式，译者应采用较正式的目的语来翻译，力求信息对应，语言规范。对于会展报告中的评论性和召唤性的内容，译者也需要运用一些编译的方法，调整语序和信息位置，加强语势，从而给读者留下深刻的印象。

例4

> Growing demand for lifestyle product in China's middle and upper classes has led to a huge surge in visitors to Interior Lifestyle China 2014. A total of 21 773 buyers attended the fair representing a very strong increase by 28% compared to the 2013 edition. These buyers came from 60 countries and regions, which was a significant increase from the 37 in 2013. The show, which featured 235 exhibitors (2013, 282) from 17 countries and regions, was held from 18 to 20 September 2014 at the Shanghai New International Expo Center across 20 000 square meters of exhibition area. While the number of exhibitors dropped this year, quality and stand sizes of exhibiting companies increased due to an adjustment in the exhibitor structure to accept increasingly mid-range and high-end companies.
>
> 2014年上海时尚家具展已于2014年9月20日在上海新国际展览中心圆满落幕。与会观众数量创下新纪录,体现出国内中高端家居市场的巨大发展潜力。创立多年以来,展会始终坚持定位于中高端生活用品市场,逐步通过结构调整提升参展企业的准入品质。为期三天的展会吸引了来自17个国家和地区的235家参展商(2013年:282家)齐聚上海新国际博览中心,整体展示面积达到20 000平方米;吸引了来自60个国家及地区(2013年:37个国家和地区)的21 773 名观众莅临参观,较去年增加28%。

熟悉文本特征
Learn about Stylistic Features

1. 词汇特征

1) 使用行业术语

会展语言以信息传递为主要功能,应当言简意赅。因此,会展文本经常使用行业术语,确保准确传达意义,避免理解上的歧义,比如,将"布展"和"撤展"分别译为"move-in"和"move-out",将"展位"译为"booth/stand",将"展区出入证"译为"Exhibition Pass",将"现场租订"译为"floor order",等等。

2) 词汇内涵丰富

作为专门用途语言,会展语言需要简洁、准确地表达意义,因此词汇的指称意义精确度高，内涵丰富。比如，会展活动可以细分为public show(公众展销会)、consumer show(消费会展)、fair(交易会)、trade fair(行业会展)、product launch(产品发布会)、workshop(现场讨论会)、symposium(座谈会)、exhibition(展览会)、exposition(博览会)、conference(年会)、convention(行业大会)、 forum(论坛)、seminar(交流会)、negotiation(洽谈会)、display(陈列会)、summit(峰会)等。

2. 句式特点

1) 使用被动句

英文会展文本经常使用被动句，以体现文本所提供信息的客观性和可信度。翻译时，译者可以根据目的语的表达需要，将英文被动句译成汉语主动句。

例5

> The New York ISA **is actually described as** a premier annual automotive event that is well recognized both nationally and internationally.
> 纽约国际车展已成为一项重要的汽车展会，每年举办一次，在国内外享有盛誉。

例6

> No pavilion shall **be put into use** without a written permission for use.
> 若无书面使用许可证，任何展馆均严禁使用。

2) 使用简略句

为了使信息表述简洁明了，会展文本常使用简略句，只呈现句子中的关键信息，以提高读者的阅读效率。

例7

> A: We are hosting an international conference on education. I thought you would be interested in sponsoring this event?
> B: **Why should we**? What will the event offer to us?
> A: 我们正准备举办一场有关教育的国际会议，我想您或许有兴趣做这次会议的赞助商？
> B: 为什么是我们？本次活动能为我们带来什么好处？

3) 使用一般现在时和现在进行时

会展文本经常使用一般现在时和现在进行时，目的是让对方产生现实感，使谈论的内容具有可靠性和客观性。

 例8

This product is now in great demand and we have on hand many inquiries from other countries/regions.

这种产品现在需求量很大，我们手头上有来自其他国家/地区的很多询盘。

 例9

It is our permanent principle that contracts are honored and commercial integrity is maintained.

重合同、守信用是我们的一贯原则。

下面通过两个典型任务来练习会展文本的翻译。

任务1. 根据提示将下面的中文会展文本译成英文。

举办中国国际进口博览会(进博会)，是中国推进新一轮高水平对外开放的重大决策，是中国主动向世界开放市场的重大举措。进博会将充分发挥"窗口"作用，推动内外循环顺畅连接，拉紧中外经济联系纽带，为各国企业提供更加广阔的市场机遇。

企业商业展是进博会的重要组成部分，自首届以来，全力推动国际化策展、综合性组展、专业化办展、分行业布展，并取得丰硕成果。专业化水平进一步提高，国际化程度进一步提升，展台内容进一步丰富，贸易和投资相互促进。

诚挚邀请全球参展企业、专业采购商、专业观众等各界人士参展参会，共享发展机遇。

(资料来源：https://country.ciie.org/)

商务英语翻译实务
International Business Translation

1. 领会翻译提示

- 会展名称采用官方说法；
- 准确翻译会展术语和经济术语；
- 一个中文句子含有多个动词，将其译成英文时，恰当选择英文谓语动词。

2. 写出英语译文

任务2. 根据提示将下面的英文会展文本译成中文。

> The 14th Annual Meeting of the New Champions of World Economic Forum (WEF) closed on June 29, 2023 in north China's Tianjin, highlighting solidarity and cooperation amid global challenges.
>
> During the three-day event, also known as the Summer Davos, more than 1 500 global attendees from businesses, governments, international organizations, and academia offered insights into topics including artificial intelligence, green transition, and climate change.
>
> This year's event takes place amid a range of global challenges, including slowing growth, debt risks, climate change, and the wealth gap.
>
> At the closing ceremony, WEF President Borge Brende said that, as the global headwinds persisted, it was more crucial than ever to engage with one another.
>
> Brende announced that the next Summer Davos will be held in China's northeastern city of Dalian. Established by the WEF in 2007, the event is held annually in China, alternating between the two port cities of Tianjin and Dalian.

（资料来源：http://www.tj-summerdavos.cn/2023davos/index.shtml）

会展文本
MICE Texts

1. 领会翻译提示

- 会展名称采用官方说法；
- 准确翻译会展术语和经济术语；
- 将一个英文长句译成中文时，采用分译法处理，确保译文层次分明、表意清晰。

2. 写出汉语译文

_____
_____
_____
_____
_____
_____
_____

接下来，我们结合上面所给的任务，具体探讨会展文本的翻译技能和方法。

依据国际会展项目流程，国际会展文本主要包括会展推广文本、会展服务文本、会展合同和会展报告。在翻译过程中，译者针对中、英文会展文本不同的篇章结构和信息排列方式，灵活运用下面给出的四种翻译方法，产出准确、简洁、专业对等的译文，实现顺畅的跨文化交流，提升我国会展企业的品牌影响力。

1. 沿用约定俗成的表达语

在翻译会展题目、主办方、承办方和媒体支持单位等专有名词时，译者要事先了解并且沿用约定俗成的表达语，不要按照自己的想法翻译，以免引起误解。

 例10

> 2023年新领军者年会
> Annual Meeting of the New Champions 2023

171

例11

主办单位：北京市文化和旅游局

Organizer: Beijing Municipal Bureau of Culture and Tourism

2. 转换词性

在会展材料翻译过程中，译者要有意识地运用词性转换法，突破原文句式格局，化阻滞为通达，准确、完整地表达原文含义，使译文符合目的语表达规范和习惯。

例12

The **implementation** of new energy vehicle program will help to increase the proportion of automobile electronics industry in automotive industry.

通过实施新能源汽车产业规划，汽车电子产业在汽车产业中的比重将持续提高。

例13

通过可持续性推动增长是在21世纪提升全球、国家与企业竞争力的基础。

Driving growth through sustainability is **fundamental** for global, national, and business competitiveness in the 21st century.

3. 调整语句结构

中文与英文会展文本分属汉、英两种不同的文化系统，形成了各自不同的文体特点。汉语文本句式整齐，经常采用对仗、排比等修辞手法，将其译成英文时要调整语句结构，进一步归纳信息，确保目的语准确、清晰、流畅。

例14

为保证本届展会的正常展览秩序，增强参展企业知识产权意识，保障参展企业及参展产品知识产权的合法权益，特制定本规定。

The regulation is hereby made up **for the purpose of keeping the order of Exhibition**, consolidating the awareness of intellectual property rights of the participants and ensuring the legal rights of them as well as their exhibits.

 例15

> The number of participants in the workshops, seminars, and discussions has also risen continuously. **Particularly well visited were** the public talk shows, which presented a summary of the results of conferences. In addition, about 45 000 people have been following the events via the Internet.
> 参加各种座谈会、研讨会和讨论会的人数也在持续上升。大量观众积极参加的公众脱口秀，成为此次会议成果的缩影。另外，约有45 000人通过互联网全程追踪本届博览会。

4. 语态转换法

会展服务信息基本上属于说明性文字，用语客观、正式且有礼貌。英文服务信息经常采用被动语句，体现客观、平实的特点，译成汉语的主动句，语气比较自然、亲切，表达效果更好。

 例16

> **It is universally acknowledged that** advance shipping enables exhibitors to confirm the arrival of their freight at the show. Additionally, freight arriving at the warehouse in a timely manner will usually be delivered to the booth during the contractor's move-in period at straight-time drayage rates.
> 人们普遍觉得，提早运输使参展商能够确保展品到达展览地。此外，及时运抵仓库的货物可以在承包商划定的入展期内以一般运价运到展台。

 例17

> **Speakers are advised to** hand in electronic presentation files to the academic service desk at least one day before their speeches. Please avoid repeated submission.
> 请发言人在发言的前一天将电子演示文件提交到学术服务台，已经提交者请勿重复提交。

国际会展文本具有鲜明的信息性特点。在翻译过程中，译者首先要努力使目的语和源语的信息对应，同时考虑两种语言在句式结构和行文习惯上的差异，适度调整语句结构和信息排列顺序，确保译文清晰、专业、流畅，达到预期的传播效果，切实提高我国会展活动的国际影响力。

1. 将下面的中文会展文本译成英文。

> 网上博览会是新兴的展览模式，通过互联网这个广阔的平台为展商提供丰富、便捷、高效的展示和推广服务。传统博览会是面对面的展示与交流，而网上博览会则是多维的，它能将文字、图像和声音有机地结合在一起，使我使众足不出户就可以身临其境般地感受品质和服务。交互性强是网上博览会的最大优势，用户可以通过网络提交个人信息、留言等，展商可以随时得到观众反馈的宝贵信息，进一步缩短了观众和展商之间的距离。

2. 将下面的英文会展文本译成中文。

> Small meetings can mean big success for organizers who have done their homework. Unlike large conferences, which require big venues usually available only in cities, small meetings offer significant flexibility of choice to organizers who are selecting an appropriate venue. And they can be more productive, with intimacy.
>
> It is vital to define carefully the meeting's purpose and to decide what you hope to achieve. This is probably the most important element in hosting a successful conference. Attractions of a beach resort are the element of fun. An appropriate venue for this type of meeting is a small hotel away from big-city attractions and beaches. If you do opt for a beach resort, it is essential to strike a balance between work and fun: allow time in the schedule for pina coladas and sun-tanning, or the attendees will not be happy.

会展文本
MICE Texts

磨炼翻译技能
Sharpen Translation Skills

1. 将下面的英文会展文本译成中文。

With the nearly 13 000m² of exhibition and convention space, the Exhibition and Convention Hall has No.1 Hall of 5 700m² on the first floor and No.2 Hall of 2 500m² on the second. It is equipped with sophisticated exhibition and conference facilities including Internet broadband access, which may provide organizers at home and abroad with full range of services. In addition, different venues for holding meetings, business talks, and technical seminars of small and medium sizes can be arranged upon the client's request accordingly on the third floor and fifteenth floor. The Convention Center has ground and underground parking spaces for both exhibitors and visitors. The Exhibition and Convention Hall has altogether 16 entrances and exits. On the first floor, there are three main entrances for visitors flow. There are also two entrances (4 meters high and 3 meters wide) on each side for goods transportation.

2. 将下面的中文会展文本译成英文。

> 大会提供8月4日、5日午餐和8月4日晚宴。请分别持午餐券或邀请函到指定区域就餐。8月6日午餐自理，可前往东方滨江大酒店(Shanghai Oriental Riverside Hotel)各餐厅就餐，或从会议中心步行5分钟至正大广场(Super Brand Mall)就餐，广场内有各类餐厅七十余家。

熟悉下面的会展文本功能句并将它们用于自己的翻译作品。

1. 布展注意事项

(1) The Organizers encourage the exhibitors to contact the Official Contractor for their own convenience.

参展商应该优先采用主办单位指定的装修代理公司,以便主办单位尽可能多地维护参展商的权益。

(2) If exhibitors employ an outside contractor, they are responsible for contacting directly the Exhibition Center.

如果参展商自己聘请其他的装修代理公司,则参展商及其装修代理公司应向展览中心提交有关申请。

(3) All stand contractors, other than the Official Contractor, must settle the onsite management fee before moving in.

除指定装修代理公司外的各装修代理公司,在入馆之前须向展览中心施工管理办公室缴纳现场管理费。

(4) Clearance of at least ×××meters between existing hall walls and stand walls is required.

展馆墙壁与展台墙壁间隔至少宽×××米。

(5) Aisle or passageway of at least ×××meters wide between rows of standard is required.

各排展台之间的通道至少宽×××米。

(6) The design and construction of booths should cause no annoyance to other exhibitors.

展台的设计和搭建以不影响其他参展商为原则。

(7) No nailing or drilling will be allowed to the Standard Booth structure.

展台上不允许钉钉子或钻孔。

(8) No freestanding fitment may exceed a height of ×××meters or extend beyond the boundaries of the site.

家具或设备在高度上不可超过×××米,或摆放在所划定的范围以外。

(9) No painting or wallpapering of the Standard Booth panels will be allowed.

不允许在展板上涂抹或粘贴。

(10) All exhibitors must adhere to these rules to ensure smooth operations on site.

所有参展商必须遵守以上各项规定，以保证展览的顺利进行。

(11) No part of any structure may extend beyond the boundaries of the site allocated.

展台的所有部分不得超越所划定的范围。

(12) No suspension can be made from the ceiling of the exhibition hall, nor may any attachment be made to the floor, walls, or any other part of the building without the approval of the Organizer.

在得到主办单位许可之前，展馆顶部不得悬挂物品，地面、墙壁或展馆的其他部分不得粘贴物品。

(13) Exhibitors who wish to construct a false ceiling must submit drawings in duplicate to the Organizers for prior approval.

参展商如希望在其展台搭建吊顶，必须预先将设计图(一式两份)交主办单位批准。

(14) Exhibitors in raw space are responsible for providing suitable floor covering, such as carpet, for their stands.

空地的参展商必须在其展台铺设地毯等覆盖物。

(15) Double layer construction should be approved by the Organizers, and additional charges should be applied.

双层搭建必须报经主办单位批准，并按规定缴纳附加费用。

2. 用电与安全保障

(1) Exhibitors should take the sole responsibility of electrical disconnection due to violation of electrical regulations.

因参展商未遵守用电规则而导致的展位断电及其他一切后果，主办单位概不负责。

(2) Electricity will be disconnected 10 minutes after the exhibition closes.

各展馆将在展览结束后10分钟准时断电。

(3) Passageways in the exhibition hall must not be obstructed with packing materials, construction materials, or debris during moving in, construction of stands or removal of exhibits.

在布展和撤展期间，不得将包装材料、装修材料和其他障碍物放置于公用通道上。

(4) The Organizers will not accept liability for loss of, or damage to, any exhibits at any time.

主办单位对布展、展览、车展期间展品的丢失或损坏不负法律责任。

(5) Exhibitors are advised to arrange for insurance, and are required to assume liability for equipment, etc., by arranging for insurance coverage.

参展商应负责自己展台的展品安全,主办单位建议参展商为其展品购买必要的保险。

(6) The Organizer reserves the right to request any company that has failed the fire safety requirement to reconstruct the booth until the requirement is met.

主办单位有权要求参展商对不符合防火安全规定的展台进行修改、重建,直至其达标为止。

3. 展台拆卸与清洁

(1) The Organizers will arrange for the general cleaning of the exhibition premises and stands(excluding exhibits) prior to the opening of the exhibition and daily thereafter, but it is the responsibility of the exhibitors to keep their stands tidy at all times.

组办单位将在开展前及每日展览结束后负责打扫展馆,但参展商有责任保持展台的一贯清洁。

(2) Exhibitors who, because of operating exhibits, are likely to have substantial quantities of waste materials for removal, must inform the Organizers in advance in order that the necessary arrangements can be made for which they will be charged.

参展商如因展品关系,需要清理大量杂物,请提前通知主办单位,以便安排清洁和缴纳费用。

(3) Moving of other stands' equipment is not allowed and will be charged double price of the moved equipment for penalty. The Organizers reserve the right to cancel exhibiting rights if exhibitors fail to follow the rule.

参展商不得随意移动其他展台的设施,否则一经查出,将处以所移动设施双倍价值的罚款。对于拒不缴纳罚款者,主办单位有权取消其参展资格。

研读党的二十大报告选段(汉英对照),提升汉英文本翻译技能,培养国际视野、家国情怀和专业能力。

全面建设社会主义现代化国家，必须坚持中国特色社会主义文化发展道路，增强文化自信，围绕举旗帜、聚民心、育新人、兴文化、展形象建设社会主义文化强国，发展面向现代化、面向世界、面向未来的，民族的科学的大众的社会主义文化，激发全民族文化创新创造活力，增强实现中华民族伟大复兴的精神力量。

In the efforts to turn China into a country with a strong socialist culture, the CPC will focus on upholding socialism with Chinese characteristics, rallying public support, fostering a new generation of young people, developing Chinese culture, and better presenting China to the world. The Party will develop a sound, people-oriented socialist culture for the nation that embraces modernization, the world, and the future, ignite the cultural creativity of the entire nation, and build a powerful source of inspiration for realizing national rejuvenation.

(资料来源：http://cn.chinadaily.com.cn/a/202210/17/WS6350b1cfa310817f312f29d6.html)

请结合党的二十大报告选段(汉英对照)，撰写本单元学习体会。

Unit Twelve
商务报告
Business Report

 Learning Goals 学习目标

- 了解商务报告的功能、构成及文体特征；
- 掌握商务报告的英汉翻译技能；
- 熟练翻译商务报告，译文准确流畅；
- 翻译商务报告时，彰显客观公正和精益求精的理念。

1. 找出与下列中文商务报告术语相对应的英文术语。

(1) 调查报告　　　　　　A. promotion report

(2) 例行报告　　　　　　B. survey report

(3) 进展报告　　　　　　C. monthly report

(4) 可行性报告　　　　　D. progress report

(5) 市场调查报告　　　　E. appraisal report

(6) 商务旅行报告　　　　F. market research report

(7) 促销报告　　　　　　G. annual report

(8) 评估报告　　　　　　H. investigation report

(9) 意见调查报告　　　　I. audit report

(10) 审计报告　　　　　 J. business trip report

(11) 月度报告　　　　　 K. case research

(12) 年度报告　　　　　 L. report description

(13) 案例研究　　　　　 M. feasibility report

(14) 报告说明　　　　　 N. research scope

(15) 调研范围　　　　　 O. routine report

(16) 建议　　　　　　　 P. conclusions

(17) 调查结果　　　　　 Q. findings

(18) 结论　　　　　　　 R. recommendations

2. 将下面的英文商务报告译成中文。

> The purpose of this report was to find a suitable warehouse in the Beijing region for our American partner. The team spent one week and found three possibilities: two situated in Tianjin, and the third in Beijing.
>
> The three common bonded warehouses are all satisfactory in terms of warehouse conditions and management level. The area of each warehouse meets the set requirement of 1 000 – 1 500 square meters in space. In addition, control of the temperature and relative humidity is also standardized.
>
> If any of the two options in Tianjin is chosen, the advantage will be closeness to the port. But the Representative Office of the American partner is based in Beijing, and there will be the problem of distance for the management. If Beijing is chosen, transportation and communication expenses between Tianjin and Beijing will have to be assessed first.

文本功能及构成
Structure and Functions

商务报告是指针对某种商务目的，向一个人或多个人提供的公正、客观和有计划的事实陈述。商务报告是日常事务活动中常见的一种公文，它以书面形式给阅读者提供有关信息和数据，分析问题，得出结论，并提供建议。许多企业(特别是上市公司、国际组织或外国机构)的各类商务报告都会翻译成英语，商务报告的翻译也显得越来越重要。

1. 商务报告种类

商务报告应用广泛，种类众多。按照其功能和内容，商务报告包括以下3种常见类型。

1) 例行报告(Routine Report)

例行报告主要用于汇报工作，即定期或不定期地向有关部门或上级领导就企业生产情况、经营状况、工作业绩等所作的汇报。

2) 调查报告(Investigation Report)

调查报告主要用于揭示事实真相，一般指受单位或个人委托，对某一情况进行调查后写出的反映客观事实的报告，以此作为委托人进行相关决策的重要依据。

3) 可行性报告(Feasibility Report)

可行性报告主要用于对可选方案进行分析、论证，最终提出论证结论。

2. 商务报告结构

依据商务报告的文体色彩，报告可以分为正式报告(formal report)和非正式报告(informal report)。正式报告一般遵循严格的格式要求，长度可以达到几十页乃至几百页。非正式报告经常以书信或备忘录的形式出现，其长度一般为1~3页，此类报告通常内容简洁，篇幅短小。这里研究的是非正式报告，它通常包括以下5部分。

1) 标题(Title)

报告的标题是整篇报告信息内容的浓缩，应该客观、准确。标题一般由名词短语构成，如UK Sportswear 2007、Investigation of the Imported Equipment等。还有一些标题由report、study等词加上修饰语构成，如 A Sales Report、A Report on the Toy Trade等。

2) 引言(Introduction)

陈述商务报告的目的、呈送对象及提交时间，也可扼要地说明报告的背景和涉及的问题事项等内容。

3) 调查结果(Findings)

列举调查和研究的结果，提出问题并分析问题。调查结果内容应当准确无误，结构清晰，语言流畅。

4) 结论(Conclusions)

对调查结果进行总结和解释，在调查研究的基础上得出结论。

5) 建议(Suggestions)

作者在经过充分论证后认为应当采取的措施或行动。一份报告的有效程度常常取决于报告所提供建议的质量高低。

熟悉文本特征
Learn about Stylistic Features

商务报告在内容上讲求客观，忠于事实；观点上要求思路清晰，引证准确；结构上要求语篇完整，布局合理；文体上讲究风格自然，语言正式。

1. 简洁明了，客观平实

商务报告在语句方面的最大特点在于其简洁性，比其他文本更加注重表达的准确性、时效性，客观描述性语句较多，不主张使用修饰、夸张性语言。

 例1

> This report includes a discussion of the investigation of the facts, conclusions, and suggestions.
> 本报告包括对事实的调查、结论和建议。

 例2

> Questionnaires were distributed to our clients for their completion at the end of a one-month period.
> 我们向客户们分发了问卷，并要求他们在1个月内完成。

2. 句式多样化

商务报告，尤其是可行性报告和调查报告，多用长句、复合句、并列复合句等句式，并通过使用介词短语、插入语、同位语、倒装句、被动语态等，使语句结构更严密，细节更突出，句子的逻辑性更强。

 例3

> The reason why I choose this plan over the other optional ones is that I find that this plan has several advantages which might be easily ignored.
> 我之所以选择这个计划而不是其他的，是因为我发现它具有一些很容易被人忽略的优势。

例4

> The main reason for the delay is that they refuse to abide by the original terms of the contract.
> 造成这次延误的主要原因是他们拒绝遵守合同上规定的条款。

3. 使用平行结构

商务报告中经常使用一些平行结构，平行成分可以是词语或句子。这类平行结构不仅简洁明了，而且可以达到强调的效果。

例5

> Our cloud business needs to further develop its AI capabilities and hone its competitive edge in enterprise services. It needs to establish a stronger presence in e-government, automotive ICT components, and safe city domains, and maintain high-speed growth with healthy gross margins.
> 我们的云服务业务要进一步增强AI能力和面向企业的服务竞争力，在电子政府、汽车ICT部件和平安城市领域增强影响力，并使销售毛利润保持稳健、高速增长。

4. 使用功能句式

一般来说，商务报告的开头会使用"This report aims/sets out to..." "The aim/purpose of this report is to..." "The report is based on..."等句式介绍报告的背景和主要内容；报告结尾会使用"It was found that..." "The following points summarized our key findings..." "The key findings are outlined below..."等来总结、揭示报告的结论。

例6

> The World Trade Report is an annual publication that aims to deepen understanding about trends in trade, trade policy issues, and the multilateral trading system.
> 《世界贸易报告》每年出版一次，旨在加深人们对贸易趋势、贸易政策问题和多边贸易体系的了解。

Business Report

例7

> As the World Trade Report 2017 outlined, technology adoption and diffusion hinge on a number of factors, including feasibility, affordability, and managerial culture, as well as legal and regulatory frameworks and public acceptance.
> 正如《2017年世界贸易报告》所述，技术使用和推广取决于若干因素，包括可行性、可承受能力和管理文化，以及法律和监管框架和公众接受程度。

下面通过两个典型任务来练习商务报告的翻译。

任务1. 根据提示将下面的英文商务报告译成中文。

Final Report on This Year's Costume Fair in Paris

To: John Brown, the Managing Manager

From: Lily Jones, the Marketing Department

Date: April 14, 2019

INTRODUCTION

This year's Costume Fair was held in Paris International Exhibition Hall from April 6 to 12, 2019. The week-long exhibition attracts more than 8 000 exhibitors from all over the world, among which our company ranks the first in the field of environment-friendly textile manufacturing of China. We feel so excited to see so many famous and outstanding brands of costumes and at the same time, the fierce competition equally touches us deeply.

FINDINGS

Since this is the first time for us to attend such a big and high-level costume fair, we find that there is huge space for us to improve.

• Our slogan is lack of creativity and novelty, and is drowned among those original and attractive brands, big or small.

• The promotion appeal does not match with our products; the theme of being environment-friendly fails to come up remarkably.

> **CONCLUSIONS**
>
> During this exhibition, we feel it is so important and vital to participate in such fairs, so as to know the latest trend in the costume field and to learn from other manufacturers.
>
> **SUGGESTIONS**
>
> Based on the experience from this fair, we'd like to make the following suggestions:
>
> • Change our slogan. We should come up with a new and suitable slogan, with both creativity and novelty, to distinguish our products from other similar brands.
>
> • Change the marketing strategies. The promotion campaign should emphasize the theme of being environment-friendly. For instance, we can add more green colors in the design of new costumes.

(资料来源：李文革. 应用文体翻译实践教程[M]. 北京：国防工业出版社，2013. 有改动)

1. 领会翻译提示

● 英文中含有非限制性定语从句，将其译成汉语时采用分译法，将非限制性定语从句单独译成一句。

● 使用词性转换法，将英文中的形容词lack译成汉语中的动词"缺乏"。

2. 写出汉语译文

任务2. 根据提示将下面的中文商务报告译成英文。

> **关于天堂游泳池问题的评估报告**
>
> **引言**
>
> 　　最近，由于顾客对我们游泳池的投诉不断增多，总经理让我调查后找出问题所在，并采取适当的处理措施。
>
> **调查方法**
>
> 　　于是，从2020年3月2日到13日，我走访了投诉的顾客并检查了大部分被投诉的游泳池。经过彻底而细致的检查，我查到了以下几个比较普遍的问题，并给出了相应的建议。
>
> **评估建议**
>
> 　　可调节的水流设定装置在达到最大速度时会卡住不动，这对于游泳技术不高的使用者来讲是个潜在的危险。水流应可以调至任意速度，以适应任何水平的使用者，这样无论是初学者还是游泳高手都能玩得尽兴。
>
> 　　游泳池不易安装，而安装后还会在底板留下裂缝。这一点有待改进，游泳池应便于安装且不需要昂贵的维护费用。
>
> 　　安装一周后游泳池里长出了绿藻。滤水系统必须改进，以保证游泳池内水质清澈，没有散发异味的化学物质。

1. 领会翻译提示

● 根据表达需要，汉语中的主动结构译成英语中的被动结构。

● 根据表达需要，翻译时调整原文语句结构，采用符合目的语表达习惯的句式，确保译文简洁明了，表意准确、完整。

2. 写出英语译文

_____
_____
_____
_____
_____
_____

　　接下来，我们结合上面所给的任务，具体探讨商务报告的翻译技能和方法。

1. 直译法

商务报告内容客观，结构完整、规范，语言清晰、简练。相应地，译者采用直译法，按照原文结构处理译文，同时兼顾目的语表达习惯，确保译文简洁流畅，从而精准传达原文的内容信息。

 例8

> The World Trade Report 2018 highlights the interplay between technology and trade. It looks at how digital technologies are transforming global commerce today, and at their implications in the years to come. This report provides a qualitative analysis of the changes that are underway, and attempts to quantify the extend to which global trade may be affected in the next 15 years.
>
> 译文：《2018年世界贸易报告》强调了技术与贸易之间的相互作用，着眼于数字技术如何改变今天的全球商业，及其在未来几年所产生的影响。本报告对正在发生的变化进行了定性分析，并试图量化未来15年全球贸易可能受数字技术影响的程度。
>
> 评析：原文开门见山地阐述了报告的主要内容，句式结构简单、清晰，充分发挥了商务报告传递信息的作用。译者采用直译法，基本上按照原文语序处理，兼顾目的语的表达习惯，译文内容紧凑，表意清晰。

2. 结构调整法

商务报告的文体比较正式，句式严谨、规范，内容完整、准确。中、英文表达方式存在差异：英语是一种形合语言，通过各种连词将语句连接在一起，句子结构严密，逻辑脉络清晰；而汉语是一种意合语言，句子之间靠意思紧密结合。因此，翻译这类语句时，译者应采用结构调整法，确保译文准确、流畅，符合目的语表达习惯。

例9

With the development of regional economy and group economy, however, it is inevitable that the developing countries including China will have more frictions and conflicts with the developed countries and the regional economic groups.

译文：然而随着区域经济和集团经济的发展，包括中国在内的发展中国家不可避免地会与发达国家及其区域集团产生经济摩擦和冲突。

评析：原文语言正式，使用了英语中常用的句式"It is +adj.+ that从句"其中，It为形式主语，that引导真正的主语，但汉语中没有此类句式。译文将that从句的主语放在句子开头，形容词inevitable译成汉语副词"不可避免地"，修饰谓语结构"产生经济摩擦和冲突"。译文通顺，表意准确。

例10

Adherence with government regulations is a basic benchmark for evaluating farmers as often the regulation in practice is below what should be enforced and implemented.

译文：评估农民的基本标准是执行政府规定，这些规定在实践中往往没有很好地贯彻落实。

评析：译文采用了结构调整法和视角转换法。如果按照原文结构将此句翻译成"执行政府规定是评估农民的基本标准，这些规定在实践中往往没有很好地贯彻落实"，译文显得前后不够连贯。把"政府规定"后移，可以使译文更加连贯。另外，below表示"低于"的意思，此处无法直译，必须转换角度，"低于"不是"没有执行"，而是"没有很好地执行"政策，所以，这里将其译成"没有很好地贯彻落实"。

3. "数据"翻译方法

商务活动中，数据使用频繁。数据可以准确表达事物的状况，可以翔实记录事物的发展状态，也可以科学地证明某些观点。在商务报告中，数据的使用比比皆是。翻译商务报告时，译者需要准确把握"数据上升""数据下降"及"数据保持不变"的表达方式，确保译文准确、简练，清晰传达原文信息。

1) "数据上升"的翻译

在英语中，表示数量增加的词语包括increase、rise、grow，"增长了多少"可以用

by表示,"增长到多少"用to表示。另外,可以用rocket、jump、leap、soar、shoot up、increase dramatically、increase sharply等表示"迅速增长"或"急剧上升"。

例11

China's actual foreign direct investment (FDI) rose by 24% to $4.58 billion in the first two months of this year while contracted FDI shot up by 37.8% in the same period.

中国今年头两个月实际外商直接投资增长了24%,达到45.8亿美元,而同期合同外商直接投资猛增37.8%。

2)"数据下降"的翻译

英语中,可以用decrease、fall、down、drop、slide、slip、shrink、dip、lessen、come down等表示数量减少,用plunge、plummet、fall dramatically表示"迅速降低""大幅下跌"。

例12

Through rounds of WTO negotiations, the average tariff rate has been reduced dramatically from nearly 40% right after the Second World War to about 4% of the developed nations and 13% of the developing countries in recent years.

经过几轮WTO谈判,近年来平均关税已从第二次世界大战后的40%大幅下调到发达国家的4%和发展中国家的13%。

3)"数据保持不变"的翻译

英语中stand at、remain at 表示数据保持在某种水平或程度上,而hover around、fluctuate则表示保持在某种水平或程度上下。

例13

China's GDP growth rate in the first half of this year was 7% — among the highest in the world — and is forecast to remain at 7% for the whole year.

中国上半年GDP 增长率为7%,是世界上增长最快的国家/地区之一,据预测,中国GDP今年全年增长率为7%。

例14

> Due to the changeable weather, the prices of vegetables fluctuate between 6 yuan and 12 yuan per kilo.
> 由于天气变化无常，蔬菜价格波动很大，每千克价格在6至12元之间。

4)"约数"的翻译

商务英语中一般不用约数，但在实际应用中难免会出现一些约数或者故意使用一些约数以促进谈判成功。英语中往往用about、around、nearly、some、roughly、more or less 等表示约数。

 例15

> This year's floods, which affect 250 million people or so and 2.25 million hectares of farmlands, have caused more than 200 billion yuan of direct losses.
> 今年的洪灾受灾人口大约为2.5亿，农田受灾面积为225万公顷，造成的直接经济损失超过2 000亿元人民币。

1. 将下面的中文商务报告译成英文。

> 例行报告
>
> 致：哈利，总经理　　自：罗伯特，培训部经理
> 日期：2021-3-23　　主题：培训
>
> 　　人事部在3月份为管理人员和普通员工分别举行了一次高级管理培训和在职岗位培训。在4月份，我们计划开一个高级培训班和3个普通培训班。如果培训人数没有增加，我们将按照原计划安排课程。
>
> 　　因为基于自愿参加的原则，所以参加两期培训班的人数不是很多。如果不不采取强制参加培训的措施，参加人数仍然会是一个问题。
>
> 　　《安全说明》的最后修订工作正在进行，封面设计和插图制作已经接近尾声，4月5日就可以发行了。

2. 将下面的英文商务报告译成中文。

Employee Wealth Report

To: President   From: Human Resources Manager

Date: June 30, 2022   Subject: The Policy of the Employee Wealth

    The materials included in this report were collected from earlier reports on personnel policies and our conventions with staff members in Robert Machinery. Many employees hope that we should formulate specific policies on employee benefits as early as possible. For all we know, other companies have such policies and our current policies have caused a lot of dissatisfaction. We propose that we formulate and practice policies at the beginning of next year.

    We would like to present these preliminary suggestions for your consideration:

(1) Everyone in the company is covered by health insurance as soon as they join our company.

(2) Those who take early retirement due to illness will have full retirement benefits if they have worked for the company for more than 20 years.

(3) Holidays are fixed at 15 days, rising to 20 days after four years.

(4) We must make sure that all personnel actions such as compensation, benefits, and transfers are administered fairly.

磨炼翻译技能
Sharpen Translation Skills

1. 将下面的英文商务报告译成中文。

> The research draws attention to the fact that in 2005 Super Chocolate's share had actually increased by 1% to 39%. However, the sales volume had decreased because the market size of chocolate dropped. Further investigations reveal that there are a growing number of people who tend to regard the milk and sugar ingredients in chocolate as bad for health. Moreover, an increasing number of rival "health candies" had appeared on the market.

2. 将下面的中文商务报告译成英文。

> 该课程为新来的销售人员和有1~3个月实地经验的销售人员而设置，培训时间约为72小时。其目的是：增加产品知识；提高与顾客打交道的效率。课程的重点在于提高销售人员与顾客打交道的能力，成功地将产品推销出去，同时在顾客中保持较高的声誉。

拓展翻译技能
Broaden Translation Skills

1. 熟悉下面的商务报告短语并将它们用于自己的翻译作品。

(1) submit the following report about...　提交的报告是关于……

(2) assess the feasibility of...　评估……的可能性

(3) focus on　重点关注

(4) according to the findings above　根据上述发现

(5) launch new products　推出新产品

(6) upon the request of...　应……的要求

(7) deal with the problem...　处理……问题

(8) explore two aspects of...　探讨……的两个方面

(9) describe some features of...　描述……的一些特征

(10) get feedback from...　从……中得到反馈

(11) examine the cause of...　调查……的原因

(12) obtain most information from...　主要资料来源为……

(13) make the following recommendations for your reference　提出以下建议供您参考

(14) present the information...　提供……的信息

(15) set out to do...　旨在……

2. 熟悉下面的商务报告功能句并将它们用于自己的翻译作品。

(1) I hope that you will pay attention to this problem and solve it as soon as possible.
我希望这个问题能引起你们的注意并能尽快得到解决。

(2) The board of directors approved your proposal at the meeting last week.
董事会在上周的会议上通过了你的建议。

(3) We have submitted this proposal to the management.

我们已经将这个建议呈交给了管理层。

(4) Please show him around our company.

请带他参观我们的公司。

(5) If possible, I would like to receive your report before the next Board Meeting.

如果可能的话,我想在下次董事会议前收到你的报告。

(6) I have dealt with the inquiry that you passed to me on Friday.

我已经解决了你周五提出的问题。

(7) I would like to know exactly what action has been taken.

我想知道你具体采取了什么措施。

(8) We suggest that the price should decrease in accordance with the present marketing situation.

依据目前的市场状况,我们建议把价格降低。

(9) Could you arrange a meeting with all the directors?

你能否安排一次全体董事会?

(10) Can you provide us with your views on how to deal with the matter?

你能否提供你对如何解决此事的看法?

(11) Please fax this information directly to me by 4 p.m. on Thursday, January 11.

请于1月11日星期四下午4点前将这些资料直接传真给我。

(12) I have several proposals for cutting down the cost.

关于降低成本,我有几条建议。

(13) Please feel free to contact me if you need further information.

如需要了解更多信息,请与我联系。

(14) Please let me know your response to these suggestions.

我想知道您对于这些建议的看法。

(15) We would appreciate hearing from you in regard to this matter.

盼望您对此事的尽快回复。

(16) As of July 1, 2015, XYZ Corporation will be implementing new policies regarding health coverage.

XYZ公司自2015年7月1日起将实行新的员工医疗保险制度。

(17) All employees must use the new accounting system by June 1, 2015.

自2015年6月1日起,全体员工须使用新的会计系统。

(18) I will be glad to discuss these recommendations with you later on and follow through on any decisions you make.

我很愿意与您进一步讨论这些建议,并遵从您所做的任何决定。

(19) I've attached my quarterly review report to this email, but I also wanted to quickly discuss the trends I've noticed in our sales data over the past few months.

随信已附上了季度报告,但我还是想在此向您简单汇报一下过去几个月公司的销售情况及发展趋势。

(20) It has come to our attention that there has been a pile of unwashed dishes that accumulates in the sink by the end of each week.

我们注意到每周末的时候水槽里面都堆积了很多没有清洗的餐具。

研读党的二十大报告选段(汉英对照),提升汉英文本翻译技能,培养国际视野、家国情怀和专业能力。

> 我们党作为世界上最大的马克思主义执政党,要始终赢得人民拥护、巩固长期执政地位,必须时刻保持解决大党独有难题的清醒和坚定。
>
> As the largest Marxist governing party in the world, the CPC must always stay alert and determined to tackle the special challenges that a large party like the CPC faces, so as to maintain the people's support and consolidate its position as the long-term governing party.

(资料来源:http://cn.chinadaily.com.cn/a/202210/17/WS6350b1cfa310817f312f29d6.html)

请结合党的二十大报告选段(汉英对照),撰写本单元学习体会。

Unit Thirteen
商务合同
Business Contract

Learning Goals 学习目标

- 了解商务合同的功能、构成及文体特征；
- 掌握商务合同的英汉翻译技能；
- 熟练翻译商务合同，译文准确流畅；
- 翻译商务合同时，彰显精益求精和客观公正的理念。

Warm-up Exercises

1. 找出与下列中文合同术语相对应的英文术语。

(1) 进口合同	A. Technology Transfer Agreement
(2) 出口合同	B. Agency Contract
(3) 销售合同	C. Import Contract
(4) 购货合同	D. Leasing Contract
(5) 寄售合同	E. Sales Contract
(6) 技术转让合同	F. Export Contract
(7) 合资经营合同	G. Purchase Contract
(8) 补偿贸易合同	H. Consignment Contract
(9) 国际工程合同	I. Electronic Contract
(10) 代理合同	J. Joint Venture Contract
(11) 租赁合同	K. Compensation Trade Contract
(12) 保险合同	L. International Engineering Contract
(13) 期货合同	M. Insurance Contract
(14) 聘用合同	N. Futures Contract
(15) 劳务合同	O. Employment Contract
(16) 许可证合同	P. Service Contract
(17) 电子合同	Q. License Contract
(18) 进口合同	R. Import Contract

商务合同
Business Contract

2. 将下列英文合同条款译成中文。

(1) Party A is a company duly organized, validly existing, and in good standing as a legal person under the laws of the People's Republic of China.

(2) The arbitral award is final and binding upon both parties.

(3) The vendor shall procure that the Purchaser acquires good title to the Shares free from all charges, lines, encumbrances, and claims whatsoever.

(4) The deposit paid by the Buyers shall not be refunded if the Buyers fail to make full payment within the time herein specified and the Buyers shall be liable for all losses incurred therefrom to the Sellers.

(5) The License herein granted is conditioned on Party B selling Licensed Devices at prices no more favorable than those followed by Party A.

文本功能及构成
Structure and Functions

商务合同是由双方或多方的当事人为了一定的事由,设立、变更或者终止各自的权利和义务关系而订立的条文或协议。商务合同内容丰富,形式各样,而且不同公司都有自己的合同制式。但是合同的结构和基本条款都是类似的。商务合同有正本(Original)和副本(Copy)之分,通常由标题(Title)、约首(Preamble)、主体(Body)和约尾(Closing)四部分构成。

1. 标题(Title)

标题是商务合同的名称,用于标明合同性质的种类,如《计算机销售合同》《仓储保管合同》《商务英语培训协议》等。

2. 约首(Preamble)

约首也称序言，包括合同编号、合同当事人、签约时间和地点、订立合同各方的地址、电话、传真及订立合同的目的等。

3. 主体(Body)

合同主体规定了签约双方的责任和义务，这些权利和义务在合同中表现为各项交易条件或条款，涉及以下几个方面：货物名称及规格、质量、数量、价格、包装、交货条件、运输、保险、支付、装运、检验、不可抗力、索赔、仲裁等。

4. 约尾(Closing)

合同的约尾要写明签订合同的双方或多方单位全称、法人代表姓名、委托代理人姓名，并加盖公章，法人代表及委托代理人也要签名、盖章。同时，约尾要表明合同份数、文字效力和附件等内容。

商务合同是社会经济发展的产物，受到法律的承认和保护。商务合同明确规定了当事人的权利和义务，一方面对当事人进行保护，另一方面又对当事人进行约束，一旦签订便产生法律效力。因此，商务合同在经济贸易活动中发挥着不可或缺的关键作用。

熟悉文本特征
Learn about Stylistic Features

1. 词汇特征

商务合同文本具有法律性质，用词严谨、精确、正式，不带个人感情色彩，以示法律语言的严肃性、强制性和权威性。下面归纳了合同英语的词汇特点。

1) 使用古体词

商务合同属于法律文本的范畴，包含古体词语，以避免重复并且反映法律文件的严谨性。古体词语通常由here、there和where加上after、by、from、in、on、to、under、upon、with等词构成。

商务合同
Business Contract Unit Thirteen

例1

> The Buyer **hereby** orders from the Seller the following goods subject to the following conditions.
> 买方据此向卖方订购下列商品，条件如下。

例2

> If either of the party fails to fulfill its obligations under this Contract, it shall compensate the other party for all its economic losses resulting **therefrom**.
> 一方如不履行本合同的义务，违约一方得赔偿另一方因此而遭受的经济损失。

2) 使用并列词语

合同英语中存在着大量的词汇并列使用现象，即同义词或近义词往往由and 或or 连接以并列使用。成对词语并列使用的现象体现了法律语言对语义准确、寓意确凿的刻意追求，因为并列成分之间通常语义交叉，可以在内容上互相补充，从而使表述更全面、严谨、富有弹性。合同英语中常见的并列词语如下：rights and interests(权益)、terms and conditions(条款)、complete and final understanding(全部和最终的理解)、customs fees and duties(关税)、losses and damages(损失和损坏)、null and void(无效)、sign and issue(签发)、able and willing(能够并愿意)、due and payable(到期应付的)、compensation or damages(补偿或赔偿)。

例3

> If the contractor shall duly perform and observe all the terms, provisions, conditions, and stipulations of the said contract, this obligation shall be null and void.
> 如果承包人切实履行并遵守上述合同的所有条款，本保证书所承担的义务即告无效。

3) 使用系指定义词

商务合同文本当事人会涉及不同的国家或地区，其语言和法律不同，各自对相同词语的解释和使用也不完全相同。为了使双方对法律文本中的概念、词语统一认识，避免歧义，有必要对协议中的关键词进行界定。这些表示定义的词称为"系指定义词"，法律文本中经常使用的"系指定义词"归纳起来有mean 和be，一般使用的形式有mean、means、shall mean、shall be，或者直接用is、are。

203

例4

"Licensed Products" are any and all the products as listed in Schedule A attached hereto and all improvements in such products which may be developed by the Licensor during the Effective Period.

"特许产品"是指合同附表A中所列的所有产品和许可方在合同有效期内可能对这些产品做的全部改进。

例5

The term "Effective date" means the date on which this Agreement is duly executed by the parties hereto.

"生效日"指订约双方签署本协议之日。

4) 使用情态动词shall

shall在法律文件中有其特殊的含义，表示"应当承担的责任和义务"，常用来表述各项具体的规定与要求，充分体现了法律文件的权威性和约束性。一般情况下，shall可直接译为"应当""必须"，也可译为"将"，有时可以不译。

例6

The quality and prices of the commodities to be exchanged between the importers and exporters in the two countries shall be acceptable to both sides and the prices shall be fixed in accordance with world market prices.

货物的质量和价格必须使进出口双方都能接受，而价格必须和世界市场上的价格一致。

例7

The Seller guarantees that the goods shall be in accordance with the Seller's specification.

卖方保证货物的品质、规格要符合卖方的规格说明。

2. 句式特点

商务合同文本规定各方的权利和义务,这就要求其语言准确、完整、可靠。因此,它的句法特点是结构复杂,句意准确、严密。商务合同英语的句式具备以下五方面特征。

1) 使用陈述句

陈述句用于阐述、解释、说明、判断和规定,语言客观平实,一般不需要渲染气氛。因为商务文书用来规定当事人的权利和义务及陈述案件事实,所以合同英语的基本句式通常是陈述句结构。

例8

> The formation of this Contract, its validity, interpretation, execution, and settlement of the disputes, shall be governed by the related laws of the People's Republic of China.
> 本合同的订立、效力、解释、履行和争议的解决均受中华人民共和国相关法律的约束。

例9

> After arrival of the goods at the port of destination, the Buyers shall apply to the China Commodity Inspection Bureau (hereinafter referred to as CCIB) for a further inspection as to the specification and quality/weight of the goods.
> 货到目的港后,买方将申请中华人民共和国国家进出口商品检验局(以下简称国家商检局)对货物的规格和质量/重量进行复检。

2) 使用完整句

为了使商务文件结构完整、表意严密,合同英语一般采用主语、谓语都具备的完全主谓句——完整句,通常不使用省略句,以免因省略而出现误解和歧义现象。

例10

> Detailed minutes shall be made for each general meeting and directors present at the meeting shall set their hands thereunto. In case of any person present by proxy, the representative shall set hand thereunto.
> 董事会每次会议,须进行详细的书面记录,并由全体出席董事签字,代理人出席时,由代理人签字。

例11

> Both parties should abide by the contract and should refrain from revising, canceling, or terminating the contract without mutual consent.
> 双方应信守合同,未经双方一致同意,任何一方不得擅自更改、解除和终止合同。

3) 使用长句

在合同英语中,通过使用完整的长句,可以准确地界定商务合同所涉及各方的权利和义务关系。这些长句往往含有许多分句或附加成分,在理解或翻译此类句子时思维要敏捷、清晰,要通过各种连接标志来理解句子含义。

例12

> The manufacturers shall, before delivery, make a precise and comprehensive inspection of the goods with regard to its quality, specifications, performance, and quantity/weight, and issue inspection certificates certifying the technical data and conclusion of the inspection.
> 发货前,制造商须对货物的质量、规格、性能和数量/重量做精密、全面的检验,并出具检验说明书,说明检验的技术数据和结论。

例13

> In addition to the purchase price, the Buyer shall pay the Seller the amount of all government taxes and/or other charges(except taxes on or measured by net income) that the Seller may be required to pay with respect to the production, sale, or transportation of any material delivered hereunder, except where the law otherwise provided.
> 除买价外,买方还得支付卖方因生产、销售或运输本合同有关商品而须缴纳的所有政府税收和/或其他一切费用(纯收入所得税除外),法律另有规定的除外。

4) 使用被动句

合同英语的文体因素和语言环境强调客观事实,应尽量减少个人感情、意愿的影响,从而使论述更客观、平实。因此,合同文本经常使用被动句,突出动作的承受者,并且对有关事项做出客观的描述。

◆例14

> The Seller shall be entitled to terminate this Contract in the event of failure by the Buyer to comply with any terms or conditions stated in this Article.
> 如果买方违反本条所规定的任何条款，卖方有权终止本合同。

◆例15

> It is mutually understood that the Certificate of Quality and Weight issued by the Chinese Import and Export Commodity Inspection Bureau at the port of shipment shall be taken as the basis of delivery.
> 买卖双方同意，以装运口岸中华人民共和国国家进出口商品检验局签发的品质和重量检验证书作为品质和数量的交货依据。

5) 使用条件句

合同英语除了规定双方应履行的权利和义务外，还考虑到各种可能发生的情况和处理办法。因此，合同文本中有较多的条件句，使条款内容更加完整和准确，避免因语用不当而导致任何一方的损失。

◆例16

> If the result of packing in cartons turns out to the satisfaction of the Buyer's clients, the Seller may continue using this packing in the future.
> 如果纸板箱包装的效果使买方用户满意，则卖方在今后的业务中可继续使用这种包装。

◆例17

> In case no settlement can be reached through the negotiation, the case shall then be submitted for arbitration. The location of arbitration shall be in the Country/Region of the domicile of the defendant.
> 如果协商不能解决，应提交仲裁。仲裁应当在被诉方所在国/地区进行。

下面通过两个典型任务来练习商务合同的翻译。

任务1. 根据提示将下面的英文合同译成中文。

> The undersigned Seller and Buyer have agreed to conclude this Contract subject to the terms and conditions stated below.
> 1. Name, Specification, and Quality of Commodity:
> 2. Quantity:
> 3. Unit Price and Total Amount:
> 4. Packing:
> 5. Shipment:
>   To be effected during _____ from _____ to _____ in two lots allowing transshipment and partial shipment.
> 6. More or less: _____ %.

1. 领会翻译提示

- 注意直译法的运用；
- 注意增词法的运用；
- 注意语态转换法的运用。

2. 写出汉语译文

商务合同 Business Contract

任务2. 根据提示将下面的英文合同译成中文。

7. Terms of Payment:

By Confirmed, Irrevocable, Transferable, and Divisible L/C to be available by sight draft to reach the Seller before _____ and to remain valid for negotiation in China until _____ after the time of shipment. The L/C must specify that transshipment and partial shipment are allowed.

The Buyer shall establish a Letter of Credit before the above-stipulated time, failing which, the Seller shall have the right to rescind this Contract upon the arrival of the notice at the Buyer or to accept whole or part of this Contract not fulfilled by the Buyer, or to lodge a claim for the direct losses sustained, if any.

8. Inspection:

It is mutually agreed that the goods are subject to the Inspection Certificate of Quality and Inspection Certificate of Quantity issued by China Import and Export Inspection Bureau at the port of shipment. The Certificate shall be binding on both parties.

9. Insurance:

Covering _____ Risks for _____ 110% of Invoice Value to be effected by the _____ .

10. Discrepancy and Claim:

In case of quality discrepancy, claim should be filed by the Buyer within 30 days after the arrival of the goods at the port of destination, while for quantity discrepancy, claim should be filed by the Buyer within 15 days after the arrival of the goods at the port of destination. It is understood that the Seller shall not be liable for any discrepancy of the goods shipped due to causes for which the Insurance Company, Shipping Company, other Transportation Organizations, or Post Office are liable.

1. 领会翻译提示

- 注意减词法的运用；
- 注意结构调整法的运用；
- 注意语态转换法的运用。

2. 写出汉语译文

_____
_____
_____
_____
_____
_____
_____
_____
_____
_____

接下来，我们结合上面所给的任务，具体探讨商务合同的翻译技能和方法。

在合同文本翻译过程中，译者往往采用直译的方法，力求忠实于原文。然而，由于两种语言在句式特点和表达习惯上的差异，常常不能照搬原文的句法，而要做出必要的变通，使译文准确、完整、严谨、规范。英文合同文本翻译的常用方法如下。

1. 词性转换

在翻译过程中，转换词性是一种常见的变通手段，它能够突破原文句式格局，化阻滞为通达，准确、完整地表达原文含义，确保译文准确、流畅，符合目的语的表达习惯。

例18

> The parties agree that any restructuring shall not **adversely affect** the economic interests of the parties.
> 双方同意，任何重组不得给双方的经济利益带来**不利的**影响。

例19

We are especially **grateful** to you for arranging the meeting for us with the Machinery Trading Delegation at such short notice.

我们特别**感谢**你们在时间那么短促的情况下安排我们同机械交易团的成员们会面。

2. 增词法

增词法指在翻译时按意义和句法的需要，增加一些词语或句子来更忠实、通顺地表达原文的思想内容，以确保译文准确、流畅，符合目的语的规范。

例20

Cargo insurance **is to** protect the trader from **losses** that many dangers may cause.

货物保险**旨在**使贸易商免受许多风险可能造成的种种**损失**。

例21

Notwithstanding **the foregoing**, a Party hereby waives its preemptive right in the case of any assignment of all or part of the other Party's registered capital to an affiliate of the other Party.

尽管有**上述规定**，如果一方将其全部或部分注册资本转让给一家关联公司，另一方则在此放弃其优先购买权。

3. 减词法

减词法是指在翻译过程中省略一些词汇的翻译方法，这些词汇在原文中是自然的、必不可少的，但在译文中却是多余的。减词法一般是出于译文语法和习惯表达的需要。

例22

The undersigned Seller and Buyer have agreed to conclude this Contract subject to **the terms and conditions** stated below.

买卖双方经协商同意按下列**条款**成交。

例23

> **We are afraid** that the L/C may expire before shipment because of the strike in our factory.
> 由于工厂罢工,恐怕在货物装运前信用证就会到期。

4. 调整语序

英、汉两种语言在思维方式和表达方式上差异很大,这也反映在词序上。调整原句的顺序旨在使译文更准确、清晰地传达原文内容,使其符合目的语的表达习惯。

例24

> The Seller shall not be responsible for the delay of shipment or non-delivery of the goods due to Force Majeure, which might occur during the process of manufacturing or in the course of loading or transit.
> 凡在制造或装船、运输过程中,因不可抗力因素致使卖方不能或推迟交货时,卖方不负责任。

例25

> All other matters related to this Contract, unless otherwise agreed and accepted by the Buyer, shall be governed by Section II, the Terms of Delivery which shall form an integral part of this Contract.
> 除非买方同意和接受,本合同的其他一切有关事项均按第二部分"交货条款"的规定办理。该交货条款为本合同不可分割的部分。

5. 语态转换法

英语合同文本强调客观事实,经常使用被动句,以突出动作的承受者,并对有关事项做出客观的描述。在翻译过程中,译者要根据表达需要,将英文中的被动句译成中文的主动句,这种译法称为语态转换法。

商务合同
Business Contract

例26

The plant, machinery and equipment, raw materials, components, and the products shall be insured by JVC for adequate replacement value against fire, storm, tempest, accident, flood, theft, and other risks which may destroy or diminish the value of the products or which may render the products unfit for consumption.

合营公司应为厂房、机器设备、原材料、部件和产品投保,一旦发生火灾、暴风雨、风暴、事故、水灾、盗窃,或出现其他可能损害或降低产品的价值或使产品不适用于消费的风险,保险获得的赔付应足以重置该财产。

例27

All disputes arising from the execution of or in connection with the contract shall be settled through friendly consultation.

双方应通过友好协商解决在合同执行过程中所产生的或与本合同有关的一切争议。

巩固翻译技能
Enhance Translation Skills

1. 将下面的中文合同条款译成英文。

在履行协议过程中,如产生争议,双方应友好解决。若通过友好协商达不成协议,则提交中国国际经济贸易仲裁委员会,根据该会仲裁程序暂行规定进行仲裁。该委员会的决定是终局的,对双方均有约束力。仲裁费用,除另有约定外,由败诉方负担。

2. 将下面的英文合同条款译成中文。

In case the Letter of Credit does not reach the Sellers within the time stipulated in the Contract, or under FOB price terms the Buyers do not send vessels to appointed ports, or the Letter of Credit does not correspond to the Contract terms, the Sellers shall have right to cancel the Contract or to delay the delivery of the goods and shall also have the right to lodge claims for compensation of losses.

磨炼翻译技能 / Sharpen Translation Skills

1. 将下面的英文合同条款译成中文。

Unless otherwise specified in the Contract, the Contract Equipment shall be packed by the Seller in new and wooden cases and necessary measures shall be taken to protect the Contract Equipment from moisture, rain, rust, corrosion, shock, and damages according to their different shapes and special features so as to make the Contract Equipment withstand numerous handling, loading, and unloading as well as long-distance ocean and inland transportation to ensure the Contract Equipment safe arrival at the Working Site without any damage or corrosion.

2. 将下面的中文合同条款译成英文。

> 乙方的报酬为税前10 000元每月，乙方在试用期的报酬为税前6 000元每月。试用期过后，甲方为乙方提供住房福利补助5 000元每月，甲方凭乙方提供的租房发票报销，报销时间在每月8日。如遇节假日或休息日，应提前到最近的工作日支付，如因特殊原因延期支付报酬，甲方应在5个工作日内向乙方说明原因。

熟悉下列商务合同语句并将它们用于自己的翻译作品。

(1) No modification of this Contract or waiver of its terms and conditions shall be effective unless they are made in writing and signed by the parties.

修订合同或取消条款条件以双方书面签字为准。

(2) The undersigned Seller and Buyer have agreed to close the following transactions according to the terms and conditions set forth as below.

买卖双方经协商同意按下列条款成交。

(3) The delivery payment shall be paid by the Buyer to the Seller under an irrevocable letter of credit.

买方应用不可撤销信用证向卖方支付运费。

(4) This Contract is executed in two counterparts each in Chinese and English, each of which shall be deemed equal authentic.

本合同为中、英文两种文本,两种文本具有同等效力。

(5) In case Party B breaches this Contract, Party A has right to deduct the default fine, compensation for damage, or any other expenses from the deposit.

因乙方违反合同的规定而产生的违约金、损坏赔偿金和其他相关费用,甲方可在保证金中抵扣。

(6) Any annex is the integral part of this Contract. The annex and this Contract are equally valid.

本合同附件是本合同的有效组成部分,与本合同具有同等的法律效力。

(7) The Seller shall not be held responsible for late delivery or non-delivery of the goods owing to generally recognized "Force Majeure" clauses.

由于一般公认的不可抗力因素而不能交货或延迟装船时,卖方不负责任。

(8) All disputes in connection with this Contract or the execution of which shall be settled through amicable negotiation.

一切与本合同及其执行有关的争执,双方应友好解决。

(9) The amount of payable royalty for the Program will be a one-time charge. The currency shall be in US dollars.

本合同采用一次性支付使用费的方式,计价的货币为美元。

(10) This Contract is in two copies, effective since being signed/sealed by representatives of both parties.

本合同一式两份,自双方代表签字/盖章之日起生效。

(11) The Seller shall guarantee that the commodity must be in conformity with the quality, quantity, and specifications specified in the Contract and Letter of Quality Guarantee.

卖方应保证货物的质量、数量和规格必须符合本合同及质量保证书的规定。

(12) Party A shall strengthen the marketing network management, standardize sale and after-sale service, and shall not provide automobile resources for unlicensed automobile distributor.

甲方应加强营销网络管理,规范销售及售后服务,对未经授权的汽车经销单位,不得提供汽车资源。

(13) If the Force Majeure lasts over three months, both Parties shall have the right to terminate the Contract.

如果不可抗力因素持续三个月以上，合同双方均有权终止合同。

(14) Without the consent of Party A, all the rights and obligations hereunder including attachments hereto shall not be completely or partially transferred to the third party by Party B.

未经甲方书面同意，乙方不得将本协议(包括附件)各项权利及义务全部或者部分转让给第三方。

研读党的二十大报告选段(汉英对照)，提升汉英文本翻译技能，培养国际视野、家国情怀和专业能力。

> 国家安全是民族复兴的根基，社会稳定是国家强盛的前提。必须坚定不移贯彻总体国家安全观，把维护国家安全贯穿党和国家工作各方面全过程，确保国家安全和社会稳定。
>
> National security is the bedrock of national rejuvenation, and social stability is a prerequisite for building a strong and prosperous China. We must resolutely pursue a holistic approach to national security and promote national security in all areas and stages of the work of the Party and the country, so as to ensure national security and social stability.

(资料来源：http://cn.chinadaily.com.cn/a/202210/17/WS6350b1cfa310817f312f29d6.html)

请结合党的二十大报告选段(汉英对照)，撰写本单元学习体会。

参考文献

[1] 鲍文. 商务英汉/汉英翻译深论[M]. 北京：国防工业出版社，2012.

[2] 陈娟. 商务英语翻译实训教程[M]. 北京：电子工业出版社，2017.

[3] 丁大刚. 旅游英语的语言特点与翻译[M]. 上海：上海交通大学出版社，2008.

[4] 丁立福. 商务英语翻译[M]. 北京：北京师范大学出版集团，2020.

[5] 董晓波. 商务英语翻译[M]. 北京：对外经济贸易大学出版社，2011.

[6] 房玉靖，马国志. 商务英语写作[M]. 2版. 北京：清华大学出版社，2021.

[7] 姜秋霞. 实用外事英语翻译[M]. 北京：商务印书馆，2015.

[8] 李玲玲. 商务英语与商务英语翻译研究[M]. 长春：吉林大学出版社，2018.

[9] 李富森，王耀强. 商务英语翻译 (家电方向)[M]. 北京：中国商务出版社，2014.

[10] 李文革. 应用文体翻译实践教程[M]. 北京：国防工业出版社，2013.

[11] 吕和发，蒋璐. 公示语翻译[M]. 北京：外文出版社，2011.

[12] 马会娟. 汉英文化比较与翻译[M]. 北京：中国出版传媒股份有限公司，2014.

[13] 潘红. 商务英语英汉翻译教程[M]. 北京：中国商务出版社，2004.

[14] 彭萍. 实用旅游英语翻译[M]. 2版. 北京：对外经济贸易大学出版社，2016.

[15] 王长春. 实用涉外酒店英语表格[M]. 北京：中国旅游出版社，2013.

[16] 徐丹. 实用商务英语翻译[M]. 2版. 北京：清华大学出版社，2021.

[17] 徐珺. 国际贸易翻译实务[M]. 北京：清华大学出版社，2018.

[18] 徐雅琴，唐沛. 应用英文大全[M]. 上海：上海科学技术出版社，2009.

[19] 苑春鸣，姜丽. 商务英语翻译[M]. 北京：外语教学与研究出版社，2013.

[20] 张炜. 外贸英语的语言特点与翻译[M]. 上海：上海交通大学出版社，2008.